NOW THE CASE FOR REINCARNATION IS STRONGER THAN EVER BEFORE.

Here are ordinary men and women recalling lives from the past—lives complete down to the most minute historical detail.

Here are people describing—in their own words—former families, lovers, enemies, and problems—as well as the sights and sounds of a past era.

Here, with the aid of hypnotic regression, are people reliving moments from another existence—laughing, weeping, sweating, screaming . . . even re-experiencing death and beyond.

"My patients and subjects have gone into previous existences to find the sources of their talents, skills, interests, strengths, and weaknesses, as well as of specific symptoms and problems. The tapestry of our lives is woven with threads that are ancient and the pattern is complex."

". . . opens a portal of fascinating possibilities."
—*Baltimore News American*

You Have Been Here Before

*A Psychologist
Looks at Past Lives*

❧

Dr. Edith Fiore

BALLANTINE BOOKS ● NEW YORK

Library of Congress Catalog Card Number: 77-20211

ISBN 0-345-32430-7

This edition published by arrangement with Coward, McCann
& Geoghegan, Inc.

Manufactured in the United States of America

First Ballantine Books Edition: February 1979
Third Printing: October 1984

Acknowledgments

I am indebted to my dear friend and fellow hypnotherapist Edgar Barnett, M.D., of Kingston, Ontario, who must have given me a powerful and unrecognized hypnotic suggestion last October when he said, "Edee, you should write a book on your work—the world needs it."

Here is the book.

It is impossible to rank in order the other people who have helped me in many different ways with this project. I owe a huge debt of gratitude to my therapy patients and those individuals who came for one session for a past-life regression. Without them there would be no book! I have learned from them as well. My husband, Greg, encouraged me from the very first time I mentioned writing this book. He has given me emotional support every inch of the way. He has spent many long hours listening to me read each chapter as it grew and offered invaluable suggestions. I appreciate my daughter, Leslie, for being so understanding and patient during the past seven months, when I was busy writing and had very little extra time. Caren McNally spent many of her weekends, even holidays, besides her regular working hours, typing the manuscript. She has been an ever-patient listener when I needed someone as a sounding board for ideas. Her steady encouragement and unflagging enthusiasm have been very supportive. Sherman Grant, my writing teacher, has helped me immeasurably. His expertise, objectivity and experience have guided me throughout in putting my daily work in a form that, hopefully, will be of interest to the reader.

I offer this book, hoping it fulfills the trust and is deserving of the support and effort of all those mentioned above.

Contents

INTRODUCTION

You Have Been Here Before

I wrote this book neither to prove nor to disprove reincarnation. Nor do I wish to settle the question of the
immortality of the soul. I am not advocating a particular method of therapy as the only or the best one. I do
want to share with you some human dramas that unfolded during two incredible years of my clinical practice—dramas of people whose current lives were crip-
pled in one way or another because of tragic events that
happened in their former lives. These people were both
my therapy patients and men and women who specifi-
cally sought to experience past-life regressions. The
growth they have made and the freedom they have
found grew out of their indomitable courage in facing,
once again, those traumas of previous lifetimes.

You Have Been Here Before is an expression of my
interests, my personality, and my background. It will be
helpful in evaluating the material that makes up the
greater part of the book if I review certain areas of my
own life.

Since the concept of reincarnation has been a basic
tenet of many of the world's major religions, I feel my
religious background is relevant here. I was brought up
attending various denominations of Protestant churches,
ranging from the Dutch Reformed to the Episcopal. My
family always lived in the country and we went to the
church nearest our farms. I do not remember ever being
taught or hearing about living more than one lifetime on
earth. In fact, in my education the emphasis was on this
as our one and only life. Both my parents are quietly
religious and believe in reincarnation, but have only recently talked of their beliefs about it. While I was a

1

deeply religious child with an unquestioning faith in God, I radically altered my beliefs during my freshman year at Mount Holyoke College when I was first exposed to agnosticism. It fitted with my scientific bent and I remained an agnostic until I began to encounter past lives through my patients' regressions. Since then I have been gradually changing most of my religious and philosophical viewpoints. At this point I am neither a staunch believer nor nonbeliever in reincarnation. However, each day as I watch more and more patients and subjects explore past lives, I find myself increasingly convinced that these are not mere fantasies.

My professional training and education in psychology was conventional, with heavy emphasis on the scientific method. Not once in the nine years I spent studying psychology—either in colleges (Mount Holyoke College and Goucher College) or graduate schools (University of Maryland and University of Miami)—was the concept, or even the word reincarnation, used. We dealt strictly in observables.

During those nine years, and despite their being downplayed by my professors, I found myself strongly attracted to the writings of Freud. I could not be deterred from the deeply rooted conviction that the way to help people was to bring to light motivations hidden deep in the recesses of their minds.

For the past eight years I have been in private practice—first in Miami and now in Saratoga, California. During these years I have seen time and time again how a person's present problems stem from subconscious factors—many times from events that are totally forgotten. Often the causative factor is deeply buried in the patient's mind; sometimes it is a feeling or attitude opposite in nature from how the person feels—or thinks he or she feels—at the conscious level. My own experience with a classical psychoanalysis during a period of marital discord proved to me firsthand that bringing subconscious material to a conscious level where it can be dealt with, using all the resources one has developed, is an extremely helpful treatment modality. But the process is slow and expensive: accordingly, I found myself searching for a shortcut to the inner mind. Through my reading I became fascinated with hypnosis as a possible answer to the problem. In looking back over those long years of education and training it seemed ludicrous to me that not once had hypnosis as a way of working with people been taken seriously. I cannot recall one lecture or one demonstration on the subject. In reaching back into my memory and mentally scanning my textbooks, it also seems appalling that the only serious mention of the technique was, at the most, a few paragraphs briefly reporting that Freud had used it initially and later given it up. Nowhere, in the standard college and graduate school texts, does it mention that at the end of his long career Freud stated that hypnosis, because of its efficiency, was the key to helping people.

The history of hypnosis as a tool of psychological healing discloses that it has been employed in many different forms since the beginning of history. The priests of the famous sleep temples of the ancient Greeks and Romans used hypnotic procedures, and hypnosis is also referred to in many passages in the Bible. After thousands of years of use in most major cultures of the world, both the British Medical Association in 1955 and the American Medical Association in 1958 gave official sanction to it and suggested that medical schools include hypnosis in their curricula.

My first exposure to the techniques of hypnosis was at a weekend seminar in self-hypnosis held at the Esalen Institute in Big Sur, California. Almost by accident I chose, on the spur of the moment, to drive down the coast to Big Sur with my brother. It started out as something exciting to share, a good chance for us to have some time together. Little did I realize that that single seminar would change the course of my life. Returning home with new skills, I asked a few patients who had worked with me for some time if they would agree to learning self-hypnosis, which I was convinced would greatly reduce their level of anxiety. They agreed, and it worked! Their success motivated me to learn more about this fascinating technique. I joined the American Society of Clinical Hypnosis, the International Congress

3

of Hypnosis and the San Francisco Academy of Hypnosis. I attended many excellent seminars for professionals and soon felt comfortable in workshops for advance students. Simultaneously, in my practice I found myself applying more and more of what I was learning at hypnosis workshops, scientific meetings and from my never-ending reading. And it was reaping rewards. Hypnotic techniques greatly speeded the therapeutic process. Thinking back over some of my complex cases, I saw that what in the past had taken years to help was often cleared up in a matter of months or even less. For me an even more spectacular development than the decrease in the number of sessions and time per case was the confidence that I could help a person to help himself or herself, the confidence that, using hypnosis, the problems could be solved and the symptoms removed.

When I first began using hypnosis I, like many other hypnotherapists, asked my patients to comb back through the years, revealing events in their growing up that caused present symptoms—resulting in the removal of the symptoms. Startlingly, a problem—for example, one of forty years' duration—could sometimes be traced back to the first months, even to the birth experience itself, which in many instances was found to be the trigger—often leaving the person feeling guilty, unwanted, and sometimes with such lifelong physical symptoms as recurring headaches. Gradually, I went back even further, discovering emotional problems arising from those supposedly cloistered months in the womb.

Now I am convinced that many problems have their roots *earlier*—in former lives. My patients and I have found that previous lifetimes can have a profound impact on current lives in terms of an individual's abilities, symptoms, relationships, character traits, and, indeed, in a myriad other ways. Until two years ago I was totally uninterested in the idea of reincarnation. Then one afternoon, while using hypnosis with a male patient, I witnessed something that radically affected both my professional life and my personal beliefs. He had come to me because of crippling sexual inhibitions. When I asked him, while he was under hypnosis, to go back to

4

the origin of his problems, he said, "Two or three lifetimes ago, I was a Catholic priest." We traced through this seventeenth-century lifetime, looking at his sexual attitudes as an Italian priest, and found the source of his sexual difficulties. I was aware that the patient believed in reincarnation. Therefore, I felt his vivid description of his past life, colored by a great deal of emotionality, was a fantasy. However, the next time I saw him, he told me he was not only free of his sexual problems, but felt better about himself in general. I began to take note of this new therapeutic "tool."

Several months later I treated a patient who worked as a social director on a cruise liner. She was very eager to solve two problems she had had for years. The first was the dangerously strong impulse she would experience to jump overboard, and the other, paradoxically, was an irrational fear of getting lost at sea. Under hypnosis she found herself as a small Norwegian boy, Sven, on his father's boat, being urged to jump as the boat crashed onto rocks. He disobeyed his father and drowned. During the same session she found herself in two other lifetimes, one as a fisherman, the other as a sailor—both lost at sea, both eventually drowning. When she came out of hypnosis, she exclaimed that she now understood both her fascination with the sea and the origin of her symptoms. Again I felt that she was "reliving" fantasied existences. I knew she, too, believed in rebirth. I still wasn't convinced. But, six weeks later, back from a trip across the Pacific, she was exuberant when she told me she no longer had either of the two problems. She had felt comfortable and free of anxiety during the entire trip.

Another opportunity to explore this area arose when a patient asked me to help her overcome her phobia of snakes. After combing back through her life under hypnosis and finding nothing to explain her fears, I tried a hunch. I asked her if she had had an encounter with snakes before she was born. She saw herself as a fifteen-year-old Aztec girl in front of a pyramid, watching priests dancing with poisonous snakes in their mouths. She trembled with emotion and reported the bizarre rites in vivid detail. Returned to the present, but still deeply hypnotized, she puzzled about what she had just experienced. She asked who she had been. She was quite distressed and stated vehemently, "I don't believe all that stuff!" Here was a person who definitely rejected reincarnation, but who had just relived a lifetime that took place four hundred years ago.

After that session I began routinely to use regression into past lives whenever, under hypnosis, the patient's subconscious mind indicated that the origin of the problem might be found in a previous existence. (Of course, in many cases the problems are the result of events in the patient's current life.)

Actually, whether the former lifetimes that are "relived" are fantasies or actual experiences lived in a bygone era does not matter to me as a therapist—getting results is important. I have found past-life regression consistently helpful, often resulting in immediate remission of chronic symptoms that do not return, even after months and years.

Symptoms and problems whose roots were traced to past lives cover a broad spectrum. For example, I now find that almost all patients with chronic weight excess of ten pounds or more have had a lifetime in which they either starved to death or suffered food deprivation for long periods. I've met "aborigines," "American Indians," "natives" of deep Africa and people from many countries who found themselves without food and often water. Starvation in past lives continues to affect the person in the present one, resulting in a compulsion to overeat. One woman patient who had a persistent fluid retention problem—one that had defied medical treatment—found herself, several lifetimes ago, dying from dehydration and starvation, as well as smallpox.

Cravings for particular foods have also been traced back to past lives. One patient referred to me by her physician had severe hypertension and was approximately a hundred pounds overweight. Time after time she—against her will—devoured bags of potato chips and other salty junk foods. This compulsion played havoc with her futile attempts to lose weight and to lower her dangerously high blood pressure. During one hypnotic regression she went back to a lifetime as a young American Indian boy who was desperately hungry because his tribe no longer had the salt to cure their dwindling game supply. Since that regression, she has not had the slightest compulsion to eat salty foods and is losing weight at a healthy rate.

Many of my patients have discovered that the causes of their phobias, fears and even aversions were rooted in some traumatic event of a previous lifetime. They have found that their irrational fears of snakes, of fire, of being alone, of flying, of crowds, of natural cataclysms, such as earthquakes and storms, derive from some misfortune in a past life.

Fear of the dark, especially, seems to originate in some terrifying incident that happened in the dark in a former life. One woman found that the origins of her phobia of staying alone at night—and her conviction that she would be murdered if she did so—came from an earlier identical experience! Another female patient was amazed to find her lifelong avoidance of train travel had its beginnings when, in her last lifetime, she saw her sister crushed beneath the wheels of a train. A young woman who couldn't bear to look at anything that was bright red (and consequently grew very anxious every Christmas) relived discovering her mother bleeding to death after having been brutally stabbed—in a former life.

Insomnia and other sleep disorders also stemmed, in many cases, from horrifying things that happened during sleep in past lives. For example, patients have relived being sexually molested or murdered while sleeping. One teenage boy who could only sleep if alone and in total silence traced his problem back to being bayoneted to death by a Japanese soldier while asleep on the sand on a Pacific island during World War II.

Headaches, pains, disorders or weaknesses of certain areas of the body were often related to events in former lifetimes, too. We have found chronic headaches, including migraines, to be the result of the patient's having been guillotined, clubbed, stoned, shot, hanged,

7

scalped or, in one way or the other, severely injured on the head or neck. Several people with chronic, intractable abdominal pains relived having their bellies run through with swords, bayonets or knives. Even the origin of menstrual problems has been traced to trauma, usually sexual, in a previous life.

My patients have been amazed to find that some recurring nightmares are actually flashbacks to experiences lived in previous lives. But we have found that pleasant events are reexperienced in dreams as well.

There are many theories concerning reincarnation and the mechanics of rebirth. One which is particularly intriguing is the concept of group reincarnation which posits that people living during certain time frames reincarnate together. For example the great thinkers of the golden age of Greece would be reborn at the same time in a new era, their talents being manifested in different ways but the links between them constant. I have been fascinated by the revelation in past-life regressions that the people we are relating to in our present lifetime we have been with before—often many times and in different roles. For example, through an exploration of former lives, patients have come to understand and sometimes resolve marital problems. One male patient with a troubled marriage found that his wife (for whom he had no sexual desire) had been his mother in a former lifetime. Parent-child difficulties, too, have been ameliorated through the insights reincarnation therapy affords. Many people have developed a greater understanding of their compatibility with their spouse or lover after examining their past life links. Instant attractions, dislikes, feelings of familiarity or distrust have been explained by events in former lives.

In my work with reincarnation theory, I am finding that there is not one aspect of character or human behavior that cannot be better understood through an examination of past-life events. My patients and subjects have gone into previous existences to find the sources of their talents, skills, interests, strengths and weaknesses, as well as of specific symptoms and problems. The tapestry of our lives is woven with threads that are ancient and the pattern is complex.

Let me share with you the dynamics of *You Have Been Here Before:* in the first chapter I show my method of regressing a person into a past life and describe patients' and subjects' reactions to exploring their previous lifetimes.

Chapters Two through Ten are case studies that include verbatim transcripts of hypnotic past-life regressions. Transcripts have been edited to avoid repetition. Names and identifying data about the patients and subjects have been changed in order to protect their privacy. Even so, I have secured permission from each person to publish his or her story.

Chapter Eleven describes the experience of dying and also includes numerous brief excerpts from transcripts that illustrate both the individuality and similarity of various death experiences.

In the concluding chapter, I discuss the questions raised for us as individuals by the concept of past lives. I also briefly share my ideas on the concepts of reincarnation and Karma.

Writing this book was a beginning for me—a beginning of crystalizing my ideas and understanding the dramas that were being played out each day in my office. I hope reading it will be a beginning for you, too. For many of you it will be confirmation of established beliefs about living again and again, and hopefully will stimulate you to begin to question yourself about the rich and varied lives you have led. For others, who may perhaps be skeptical, I hope it is a beginning of exploring a new way of looking at ourselves, either as having lived before or as having the most creative imagination conceivable.

CHAPTER ONE

❈

"Close Your Eyes and . . ."

What is it like to experience a past-life regression? I invite you to follow the steps.

My consultation room is a one-story professional building shared by psychotherapists. It has one wall of glass overlooking a wooded area. Immediately outside are sycamore trees and wild flowering shrubs, with a small creek an easy stone's throw away. Large black-crested Stellar's jays, green hummingbirds, a pet gray squirrel and a doe and her fawn are daily promenaders in front of my window-wall. Invariably the first comment a newcomer makes on entering my office and looking out the window is, "How beautiful and peaceful!" Everyone seems delighted with the view and especially the antics of the squirrel and her two babies. At times this scene can be very distracting—for this reason I shall sit facing you with my back to the outside!

After you have settled yourself in the Danish reclining chair, I ask you what you would like to find out about yourself. Since you have come for a past-life regression, not as a patient for therapy, your reasons may be fairly vague. Usually the answer is, "Oh, I'd just like to know who I was before." At this point I offer the "menu"—various topics from which you can select. Sample items are exploring a past-life relationship with a partner or family member, finding a lifetime in which a talent or skill was highly developed, the first incarnation on earth, the last one and/or a life as the opposite sex. If you have a special interest or hobby, such as a fascination with Victorian houses, the Revolutionary War, racing cars, sailing, then you might choose to investigate its origins.

After we make a decision on at least two areas of interest, I find out how you feel about being hypnotized. Most people have a deep fear of giving up control to someone else. They are also worried about losing consciousness and not knowing what is happening. As one person put it before his first hypnotic induction, "Someone else takes over and you lose yourself completely." My first task is to dispel these fears and help you view the regression as an exciting adventure. I explain to you that you will not lose consciousness, as you do while sleeping. Your conscious mind is always aware of what is going on, both within and without. In the beginning of the trance, and sometimes well into it, you may notice noises in the hall or outside of the room, but gradually you will focus more and more on the unfolding inner drama. Your conscious mind may doubt, question or revel in the scenes that develop. Of course, you are always aware of me, to some degree. Sometimes after coming out of the trance, people have reported wondering who that voice belonged to. Some are aware that it is I and even address me during the regression. Others respond to the voice, but pay no particular attention to it. It is just there, accepted. One patient, regressed to a lifetime as an American Indian girl, studying herbal medicine, became very evasive and finally announced determinedly, "I do not want to talk to you anymore!" Still under hypnosis, but back in the present, she explained that, as the Indian girl, she felt I was a "test." Since the herbal cures were secret, she became really frightened of me. Also, she could not understand who was asking those threatening questions. When I tried to explain, we got lost in a hopeless tangle. Then and there, she refused to speak another word, even folding her arms across her chest to accentuate her decision.

I point out to you that you are always in control of the situation—sometimes with the conscious part of your mind, but always with the subconscious.

I begin the hypnotic induction by asking you to recline back in the chair. Then I suggest that you close your eyes and focus your attention on your breathing.

When you show signs of beginning to relax, I ask you to use your imagination and "feel the relaxation from your closed eyelids flow out onto your temples like a warm, relaxing liquid." I direct your attention to its spreading over, and relaxing, one by one, the muscles of your face, and then progressively those of your whole body. This takes about ten minutes. I ask you to imagine yourself lying down in your favorite place in nature and, using the various senses—one at a time—to experience the scene and yourself in it. This is an easy way for you to prepare to experience the scenes that will develop during the regression.

By now, you are in a deep enough trance for a past-life regression, *but* there are still two important steps. I set up finger signals by asking you to think the word "yes" over and over and to notice that "a finger lifts all by itself—lifted by the subconscious mind." A "no" finger and an "I don't want to answer" finger come next. Then I ask the inner mind, or subconscious mind, if it is willing for you to go back to a former lifetime. If we get a "yes" response, we proceed directly.

Sometimes there is a great, almost insurmountable resistance from the subconscious mind to regress—and often for very valid reasons. For example, after many months of resisting anything more than a light trance, a patient finally found herself on an operating table in a psychiatric hospital. The surgeons were performing a pre-frontal lobotomy on her. She bled to death as they walked out, having given up. After surfacing the origin of her fear of "going under" and allowing someone to work on her brain, she has regressed to many past lives with ease—and is solving her problems and eliminating her many symptoms.

If your subconscious indicates that there is some resistance to regressing, I then bargain with it. I offer a way of viewing the material that puts distance between you and the experience. I suggest that you will see it portrayed on a "movie screen" in your mind. If need be, I suggest a posthypnotic amnesia if you cannot handle certain aspects of what will emerge. This arrangement agreed upon, I regress you to a former life by counting to ten very slowly, suggesting that you go back in time and space through a time tunnel—and at "the count of ten you will find yourself in another time and another place in another body, but it will be you." I suggest that the images and impressions will be very clear and vivid. By then you usually start to move your closed eyes, grimace, look puzzled or in some individual way convey to me that you are experiencing something. I start questioning you and you are able to answer—in English. Sometimes it takes a bit of prodding on my part for the images to emerge and for you to find yourself "there."

People experience regressions in many different ways. I have found that if they experience one past-life regression vividly with all five senses, they will usually experience all past lives very similarly. Some just describe seeing themselves, as though viewing a movie. Others fully relive every second. Some remain calm and unemotional, even while describing being raped, scalped or burned at the stake. Others shout, cry or scream. I find it fascinating to see how one person reacts as different personalities in different lifetimes. Most of my patients and subjects are consummate "actors" as they portray their various roles. During the regression, many people get so much into the character that they do not understand certain words I use, such as "year," "custom" and "country." In these cases, I suspect that their conscious minds are really "not in the act" at all. So far, I have not had anyone speak in a foreign language. Lately, though, just to be on the safe side, before regressing subjects, I suggest that they will speak to me in English.

Some people are very definite about names, dates and places, while others are confused or get lifetimes mixed up. For example, in one regression, I asked a patient who she was and she hesitantly said "Tia"— then as she got into the lifetime a little more she corrected herself, recalling another name. In another regression she found herself clearly as Tia. I usually can tell when there is confusion by the way a question is answered and, of course, if it makes sense in terms of what happens as the regression progresses.

After progressing through the significant events in the former life, I take you through your death and into the state immediately following the dying experience. Like all other painful or traumatic experiences, people experience it differently—apparently according to their capacity to tolerate stress. I may need to help you by giving you calming suggestions through your death or any other unpleasant events.

After we have gone through the life we wanted to look at or have dealt with the material responsible for a problem, I give you suggestions to return, still remaining deeply relaxed, to the present and to yourself, mentioning your name. I count backwards from ten to zero. Once back, we discuss what you have just experienced. You may add interesting details, such as correcting "lies" that the "other" person told, or filling me in on details or feelings that were hard to describe at that time. I ask you if any of the people you interacted with are people you know in this lifetime. Sometimes you may feel uncertain. If so, I give you suggestions that help to make it very clear. At this point, I ask your inner mind to reveal to you all the ways in which the lifetime you have just explored has affected you in your present life. Often interests, fears, and other facets of one's personality are due to unsuspected causes that can very easily be overlooked. Just before I bring you out of the trance, I give you suggestions that you will feel "really good and remember everything and within the next few days receive more and more insights about that lifetime." I slowly count to three and ask you to open your eyes. Often people open their eyes, frown in disbelief and say, "But I didn't go anywhere! I was here all the time." We then talk over what you have experienced and what it means to you.

In this chapter, I have described my hypnotic techniques. Now, I would like to make it very clear to you that there are dangers involved.

I cannot emphasize too strongly that I feel past-life

regressions—and even regressions to an earlier period in the current life—should be done *only* by a person well-trained both in hypnosis and psychotherapy. Multiple personalities, severe depressions, unmanageable feelings of guilt, great physical discomfort—all, and other more minor effects—have been felt by people after they have gone through a past-life regression. These symptoms *must* be treated with utmost skill.

CHAPTER TWO

"Someone's Got a Club"

The first time I saw Becky I was struck by her delicate, childlike appearance. She looked more like a sixteen-year-old than a young woman of twenty. Soft freckles, fine light brown hair and a petite figure accentuated the impression of budding femininity. She was neatly dressed in blue jeans and a colorful hand-embroidered Indian blouse. In a small, barely audible voice that trembled in unison with her body, she tried to explain why she was seeking help. Her chin quivered as she looked at me with pleading eyes, unable to continue. I suggested she make herself comfortable, settle back in her chair, put her feet up on the ottoman and take some deep breaths. We had plenty of time to deal with her problems. First things first. After a few moments of concentrating on her breathing, she was composed enough to continue.

She explained that she had had "terrible headaches" for years—since she was thirteen. When one struck she would be sick for days, usually vomiting and having to go to bed. Aspirin and migraine medication were part of her armamentarium. Her family physician had referred her to me because he suspected her headaches were due to tension and he felt she needed to learn to relax. Becky agreed that she felt tense most of the time. She laughed nervously as she counted off the ways in which she was "uptight." She found college too demanding because of deadlines, exams, papers. She had problems with her boyfriend. Her job got to her—and on and on.

She looked down at her folded hands for a few moments and then, looking up at me, reported matter-of-factly, "Mom told me to tell you I can't have a climax."

16

Becky said she thought at first it was because she was not used to having sex and that she and her boyfriend, John, would eventually feel more comfortable with each other. Then she would be more responsive. But month after month, it was just the same. "Not exciting at all." As with many couples, her lack of responsiveness was adding to the tension. Initially each secretly "blamed" the other. As time passed, her boyfriend admitted he felt extremely inadequate as a lover. She, of course, felt like a failure.

Becky's face brightened when I asked her about her home life. Her view of her family was suspiciously idealized. Her father was "perfect." Her mother was warm and loving. Her sisters were good friends. They all got along fine. I had the feeling she was hiding some pretty uncomfortable feelings from herself. I sensed I would have to wait before probing in this area.

During the last twenty minutes of our session I taught Becky self-hypnosis, making a tape for her to use at home. She was a difficult subject, keeping her eyes open as long as possible. Then, after finally relaxing her lids and letting them close, she opened them again. Obviously, part of her was struggling against surrendering to the irresistible need to relax and let go. Eventually, most of the tension drained from her face and body as she listened to my suggestions to relax the various muscle groups one by one. Finally she relaxed sufficiently for me to establish finger signals—setting up communication directly from her subconscious mind. Within minutes her inner mind indicated that her headaches were due to an event from the past. "Did this event occur in this lifetime?" Her "no" finger trembled as it slowly lifted. I asked her inner mind if it were willing to prepare her at a subconscious level to deal with the lifetime responsible for her headaches between now and our next meeting in two weeks. Her "yes" finger lifted after a suspenseful thirty seconds.

Out of the trance, Becky looked at me quizzically. "What does that mean?" I explained to her that I have found that some people's symptoms have origins in their past lives. She said she wasn't sure she believed in reincarnation. I asked if she would be willing to see what her subconscious revealed to us next time—just by keeping an open mind. She agreed with a hopeful smile and a nod. She left after agreeing to practice self-hypnosis at least twice daily.

Two weeks later, when I walked out to the waiting room to greet her, I saw a changed young woman. She seemed happier and more relaxed. Once settled in my office, she beamed, saying she liked using the tape. Even her boyfriend liked it! And now he was more relaxed, too. But she began to become tense as she asked me if we would go back into a past lifetime during that session. I suggested that we leave that up to her inner mind to decide.

As I started the induction, I could see the weeks of practice paying off for her as she slid into a profound trance within a few minutes. A check with her finger signals again pin-pointed our target as an event in a former life. I led her back through time and space, suggesting she go back to a pleasant or neutral event in the lifetime we needed to explore.

Becky's voice became even softer as she described what she was seeing:

B. There's all kinds of wildflowers—tall grass . . . in a field.

DR. F. What are you doing in the field?

B. I'm with a friend.

DR. F. Tell me about your friend.

B. It's a guy . . . I think we're just talking.

DR. F. How do you feel?

B. Good.

DR. F. You feel good toward him?

B. Yes. Relaxed.

DR. F. Tell me about the countryside. What do you notice?

B. There's a meadow, and a clearing. Trees.

DR. F. What kind of flowers do you see?

B. Orange ones, and they're little tiny . . . it's like spring . . . orange and lavender.

DR. F. Tell me about your friend. What does he look like?

B. Umm . . . dark hair . . . beard, goodlooking.

DR. F. What is he wearing?

B. It's like some kind of medieval . . . looks like tights . . . and a shirt . . . expensive.

DR. F. What color is the shirt?

B. Mauve . . . with white underneath.

DR. F. What color are his tights?

B. Gray.

DR. F. What about you? What are you wearing?

B. Green . . . solid green dress.

DR. F. How is your hair done?

B. It's pulled back at the sides and on top and—it's kind of long and flowing in the back.

DR. F. Are you really good friends, you and this young man?

B. Um-hmm.

DR. F. Are you in love with each other?

B. I think so.

DR. F. All right. Now I'm going to count from one to three and on the count of three you will be able to know his name. One . . . two . . . three . . . and whatever comes to mind, just speak out.

B. Ian.

DR. F. Okay.

B. [Laughing.]

DR. F. Why is that funny?

B. Because it just seems so strange. I never knew anyone named Ian.

DR. F. What is your name?

B. I don't know.

DR. F. Concentrate on your breathing and I'm going to ask again. One . . . two . . . three . . . and what comes to mind?

B. Elaine?

DR. F. What's your last name, Elaine?

B. O'Donnell.

DR. F. Just relax deeper and deeper. Elaine, how old are you?

B. Fifteen.

19

DR. F. Fifteen? And how old is Ian?

B. Sixteen.

DR. F. Have you known each other a long time?

B. Yeah.

DR. F. And what country are you in?

B. England? . . . Ireland. I think, England.

DR. F. Now I'm going to count to three and on the count of three the date will occur to you. One . . . two . . . three. What comes to mind?

B. Sixteen fifty-four.

DR. F. Sixteen fifty-four. Now let's just move ahead in time five or ten minutes and see what happens at the count of five. One . . . two . . . three. . . four . . . five . . . and what comes to mind?

B. Nothing's changed.

DR. F. Are you still there, talking?

B. Um-hmm.

DR. F. Are you standing up or sitting down or lying down?

B. Well, we're lying down on our sides. Relaxing.

DR. F. All right. Now I'm going to ask you to move ahead an hour or so. One . . . two . . . three . . . four . . . five.

B. Well, I'm not there anymore.

DR. F. And what are you aware of?

B. I'm in a . . . I guess it's my home . . . in the kitchen, I guess.

DR. F. What are you doing?

B. I think we're going to eat dinner.

DR. F. And tell me about your kitchen. What does it look like?

B. Well . . . it has a big wooden table with benches on either side.

DR. F. Tell me more. Is the table set?

B. We're setting it. The plates and . . . everything's metal. I don't know what kind or what quality, but it's clean.

DR. F. And how many places are you setting?

B. It's hard to say . . . I think four or five.

DR. F. And whom are they for?

B. My parents and my sisters.

20

DR. F. How many sisters do you have?

B. Two.

DR. F. Are they younger or older than you?

B. One's older and one's younger.

DR. F. What are their names?

B. Susan? . . . Emily?

DR. F. In a few moments I'm going to ask you to move ahead to the middle of the meal so that you can see what you're eating and tell whether you enjoy it. One . . . two . . . three . . . four . . . five. What comes to mind?

B. Chicken . . . it was cooked whole . . . got like legs and stuff.

DR. F. What else are you eating?

B. Some kind of mush, white stuff.

DR. F. Do you like it?

B. Yeah.

DR. F. Anything else?

B. There's a vegetable of some kind.

DR. F. What color is it?

B. Green. I think it's asparagus.

DR. F. And what is the atmosphere like?

B. It's happy.

DR. F. Tell me about your father and mother. What do they look like?

B. My father is heavy . . . kind of red-faced . . . brown hair . . . bald on the top.

DR. F. What does he do for a living?

B. He works in the town. I think he's got a store or something.

DR. F. What does your mother do all day?

B. She's at home.

DR. F. And what do you do during the day?

B. I work.

DR. F. What kind of work do you do?

B. I think I work in my father's store.

DR. F. All right. Now I'd like you to move ahead to the next significant event. Your inner mind will select the event we need to look at. One . . . two . . . three . . . four . . . five. And what are you aware of?

21

B. [Silence.]

DR. F. What are you experiencing?

B. Confusion.

DR. F. All right. I'm going to ask your inner mind to clear up the confusion at the count of five and you will know clearly where you are at the next significant event. One . . . two . . . three . . . four . . . five . . . and what comes to mind?

B. Somebody's going away.

DR. F. And who is that?

B. I think it's. . . Ian.

DR. F. Where are you now, Elaine?

B. I'm working.

DR. F. Are you in the store?

B. Yes.

DR. F. Is Ian there in the store too?

B. No. I think he's gone. [With a note of sadness.]

DR. F. Where did he go?

B. I see soldiers.

DR. F. He's with the soldiers?

B. I think . . . yeah . . . he went with them.

DR. F. Is Ian a soldier?

B. Now he is!

DR. F. How do you feel about that?

B. Upset, but I'll be all right. [Tears forming.]

DR. F. How old are you now?

B. Sixteen.

DR. F. Now I'm going to ask your inner mind to take you to the next significant event at the count of five. One . . . two . . . three . . . four . . . five. What are you aware of?

B. Hmm . . .

DR. F. How are you feeling?

B. Uncomfortable. [Her chin quivers.]

DR. F. You're uncomfortable?

B. Um-hmm.

DR. F. Why is that?

B. There's something frightening going on.

DR. F. And what is that?

B. I don't know. There are a lot of people running around.

22

DR. F. Where are you?

B. Out in the street.

DR. F. And people are running?

B. Um-hmm.

DR. F. What else do you see?

B. Horses.

DR. F. Listen and see if you can hear what the people are saying.

B. They're saying to clear the street. [Sounding frantic.]

DR. F. And why is that? What do you suppose has happened?

B. I don't know.

DR. F. How do you feel inside yourself?

B. Scared . . . confused . . . but I don't understand why.

DR. F. Are you there by yourself?

B. Yeah . . . well. Yeah, I'm at the store . . . and I don't know where my family is.

DR. F. All right. I'm going to count from one to five and I'd like you to move ahead in time a few minutes to see what happens. One . . . two . . . three . . . four . . . five. What comes to mind?

B. Someone important just went through town. [Turning her head as though watching movement.]

DR. F. Who was that?

B. Some kind of royalty.

DR. F. Now I'm going to count to five and at the count of five you will know exactly who it is. One . . . two . . . three . . . four . . . five and what comes to mind?

B. Prince.

DR. F. Prince who?

B. I don't know.

DR. F. Tell me more about him.

B. Nobody likes him.

DR. F. All right. Now I'm going to ask your inner mind to take you to the next event and perhaps this will be the event that has to do with your headaches. At the count of five, staying calm and relaxed, one . . . two . . . three . . . four . . . five, what are you experiencing?

B. Nothing.

DR. F. What are you aware of?

B. [Long pause.] My hands feel cold. This hand feels like it's asleep and I don't know if that's real or not.

DR. F. Where are you, Elaine?

B. I don't know.

DR. F. Are you inside or outside?

B. Inside.

DR. F. How old are you now?

B. Sixteen . . . same age.

DR. F. What is happening?

B. Something's changed.

DR. F. Something's changed?

B. Everything's changed.

DR. F. Everything has changed. Tell me more about that.

B. I don't see anything . . . but I feel like . . . I'm alone somewhere.

DR. F. What are you doing? Are you sitting up or lying down or . . . ?

B. Standing.

DR. F. Tell me more about that. Are you in your father's store?

B. No.

DR. F. Where are you standing?

B. It's dark or . . . or else I just can't see anything.

DR. F. But you have the feeling that everything has changed?

B. Yeah.

DR. F. Tell me more. What are you aware of?

B. No, I'm not really—I don't feel scared.

DR. F. How long ago was it that you had to clear off the street?

B. Months.

DR. F. Months ago? Now I'm going to count one to five and you will go back in time a little to just before that event. One . . . two . . . three . . . four . . . five, and whatever comes to mind, just speak out.

B. I'm being taken . . .

DR. F. You're being taken?

B. I can't—I can't tell if I—yeah, I went somewhere.

24

DR. F. Where did you go?

B. I think I didn't really want to go.

DR. F. Who took you?

B. . . . on a horse.

DR. F. You were on a horse?

B. I don't know.

DR. F. Tell me about that. What do you remember about being taken? Where were you when you were taken?

B. I was in the town . . . on the street—after the prince rode by.

DR. F. The same day?

B. Yeah.

DR. F. And what happened? What comes to mind? I'm going to count from one to three. One . . . two . . . three.

B. Someone put me on the horse.

DR. F. Who would do a thing like that? Why?

B. A soldier. [Her whole body trembles.]

DR. F. A soldier just came and took you?

B. He was with the rest of them.

DR. F. And how did you feel when that happened?

B. Surprised . . . but I don't feel like I'm all upset. [Becoming calmer.]

DR. F. What did he say to you as he took you?

B. [Silence.]

DR. F. I'm going to count from one to three and on the count of three you will know what he said. One . . . two . . . three.

B. That I was going with . . . said, "You're comin' with . . . the other women."

DR. F. You're coming with the other women?

B. They had other women.

DR. F. Did they take the other women the same way?

B. They—they wanted to go. I see women in cloaks, you know, with little bundles all packed up.

DR. F. What are you wearing?

B. Red. Red dress . . . heavier, I guess it's a different season, colder.

DR. F. Okay. Now I'm going to ask you to move ahead to the next significant event at the count of five.

One . . . two . . . three . . . four . . . five . . . and what comes to mind?

B. A dark room.

DR. F. You're in a dark room? Tell me more.

B. I'm alone. . . there's a small window . . . at least one . . . all I can see right now.

DR. F. What are you doing in the dark room?

B. Just standing.

DR. F. Are you at your home?

B. I'm trying to figure that out.

DR. F. I'm going to count from one to three and on the count of three you will know. One . . . two . . . three.

B. Not, it's not home.

DR. F. Where are you?

B. In a very large stone building.

DR. F. How long have you been in this one room?

B. Months.

DR. F. Are you being kept prisoner there?

B. Kind of. I think . . . I think so, but I've never really tried to get away.

DR. F. Why is that?

B. Well, it's better than home.

DR. F. In what way is it better than home?

B. It's more exciting. [Smiling weakly.]

DR. F. Tell me what happens. What happened to you after you were brought there by the men, the soldier on the horse?

B. We were given rooms.

DR. F. And tell me more about how you were treated.

B. We were treated well, but I think we were there for the soldiers' entertainment.

DR. F. What do you mean by that?

B. Well, like they could come and see us any time they wanted.

DR. F. And how did you feel about that?

B. I resented it!

DR. F. Now tell me what happened when they came and saw you.

B. Well . . . they were like soldiers . . . been away a long time . . . they wanted women.

26

DR. F. And how did you feel about that?

B. It was something to do. [Said matter-of-factly.]

DR. F. Had you ever been with a man before? In that way?

B. No.

DR. F. And what was it like for you the first time?

B. Indifferent.

DR. F. It wasn't very upsetting for you?

B. Ahhmmm . . . it was upsetting but . . . not earth-shattering.

DR. F. Now I'm going to ask you to move ahead in time. One . . . two . . . three . . . four . . . five. Have you been away for some time, Elaine?

B. Um-hmm.

DR. F. How long has it been?

B. Six or seven years.

DR. F. How have these years been for you?

B. Hmm . . . they've been all right. They haven't been, well . . . I've been well taken care of . . . but, they've been . . . just haven't been really enjoyable. They had their good points and their bad.

DR. F. During these years have you had any children?

B. No.

DR. F. During these years did you have one special lover or have you just been kind of used by most of the men?

B. Most of the men.

DR. F. How do you feel about that?

B. Resentful. [Her mouth tightening up.]

DR. F. Have you had any enjoyment out of it?

B. Some.

DR. F. Did it get easier after you got used to it?

B. Yeah.

DR. F. What about the prince? Were you ever with him? Did you ever get to know him?

B. No.

DR. F. Were you ever in his presence or his company?

B. No.

DR. F. Were you housed with other women? Or did you have your own place?

B. We had our own rooms.

27

DR. F. Now move ahead to the next significant event. One . . . two . . . three . . . four . . . five. What are you aware of?

B. Home.

DR. F. Tell me what you see.

B. Kitchen . . . big wooden table, benches.

DR. F. And why are you home?

B. To find my family.

DR. F. Did you have any trouble leaving where you were?

B. No.

DR. F. And have you found your family?

B. No, they're not there. [Sounding puzzled.]

DR. F. Are there any notes or messages?

B. No.

DR. F. Is the place in order or does it look like something happened in a hurry?

B. Well, it's not in a shambles, but it does look like something happened in a hurry.

DR. F. Okay, and what comes to mind? Where do you think your family is? What do you think might have happened?

B. They must have had to leave fast . . . get away from something. [Worried.]

DR. F. What could that be? What's going on in the country at this time?

B. Well, unrest. There's a lot of unsettlement. They might have had to leave. There might have been soldiers.

DR. F. And now what are you doing? Are you walking around the house?

B. Yeah, and I decide to go over to the store and see if it's still there.

DR. F. How far is the store from the house?

B. About a block.

DR. F. Tell me what you're doing.

B. I'm walking down the street—to get to the store.

DR. F. What kind of store does he have?

B. General type things. Some cloth and flour—small amount of metalware, things like that. Small store.

DR. F. Do you see any old friends or neighbors?

B. I see . . . no one. [Gripping the arms of the chair.]

DR. F. Is that unusual?

B. Yeah.

DR. F. What comes to mind?

B. [Slowly.] They all must have had to leave also.

DR. F. And how do you feel, being there alone?

B. Frightened. I don't understand. [Her voice quavers.]

DR. F. Tell me step by step what's happening. Are you walking there now?

B. I'm walking and the door's open and that's strange . . . and I'm looking around and I'm calling out. No one's answering. So I step outside in the back, I guess.

DR. F. What is the back like?

B. It's a narrow alley. It's wet and smelly. [Putting her hand to her nose.]

DR. F. Why is it wet?

B. Sewage . . . there's no one out there.

DR. F. No one's there either?

B. I can't see anyone.

DR. F. Now what are you doing?

B. I'm thinking.

DR. F. And what are you thinking?

B. I'm trying to think what to do next . . . so I close the door and go back inside . . . there's no money.

DR. F. You check that?

B. Um-hmm.

DR. F. Where did you look?

B. In the drawer—behind the desk . . . it's not—the place doesn't look ransacked, so I just think they left for somewhere.

DR. F. Stay calm and relaxed, become more and more relaxed with each breath. What are you doing now?

B. Now I'm walking out of the store.

DR. F. And are the streets still empty?

B. Yeah . . . I can hear dogs, but not very many . . . I can't find any people. [Now obviously upset.]

DR. F. And how are you feeling?

B. Frightened. I'm beginning to be very frightened. I don't know where everyone is.

DR. F. Just stay relaxed and calm. And now what are you doing?

B. I stopped walking around, trying to find someone.

DR. F. Whom were you looking for in particular?

B. Anyone.

DR. F. Did you know most of the merchants and other people there in town?

B. Um-hmm.

DR. F. And now what happens?

B. [Lowering her voice.] I hear footsteps.

DR. F. Somebody's walking?

B. More than one. Sounds like men. [Breathing rapidly—her face flushes.]

DR. F. Are they in back of you?

B. Um-hmm. [Trembling violently.]

DR. F. How do you feel when you hear those footsteps?

B. Frightened because, if . . . if they were people that I knew they wouldn't be walking up so fast behind me without saying anything . . . no greeting . . . so I keep walking. They catch up with me.

DR. F. Tell me what you're experiencing. What do you see?

B. I see three men. Their faces are blurred.

DR. F. I'm going to count from one to three and the faces will become very clear to you. Just relax, take a deep breath—really deep breath, now. Exhale and just let out any tension. One . . . two . . . three . . . and what comes to mind?

B. One's fair—blond hair . . . the other's dark with a moustache . . . another dark one—but no moustache.

DR. F. What are their expressions?

B. Well . . . they're angry-looking.

DR. F. Do they say anything to you?

B. No.

DR. F. Are they touching you?

B. [Tears flowing down her cheeks.]

DR. F. What are they doing?

B. One is grabbing my arms from behind . . . they've pulled me in between two buildings, dropped my bag . . . my cloak.

30

DR. F. Do they say anything to you?

B. No, they're talking to themselves—to each other. [Great tension in her body.]

DR. F. What are they saying?

B. Oh, you know, "Quick, quick, get her back here." They're telling me, "Be quiet!" . . . to each other and to me. One man's got his hand over my mouth.

DR. F. How do you feel?

B. Hmm . . . I'm frightened because I think they might hurt me. But—I've been with a lot of men, outside of my own choice, so that part doesn't really . . . more of the same. But this time I'm frightened because they really might hurt me . . . and I don't know them.

DR. F. And now what happens?

B. Someone's got a club of some kind—metal . . . Ohhh . . . they hit me on the head, because I'm struggling . . . I fall, they let me fall. [Her body goes limp.]

DR. F. Does it hurt badly when they hit you on the head?

B. Yes. I think they cracked . . . blood . . . they hit me again. [Sobbing violently.]

DR. F. Where do they hit you this time?

B. On the other side of my head.

DR. F. Are you down on the ground now?

B. [Groaning.] . . . Yes.

DR. F. They're standing up?

B. Yes . . . no, now they're getting down—on their knees, sitting—they're deciding who's going to rape me first . . . I'm only semiconscious.

DR. F. What do they say?

B. Oh, they're just arguing. "Me first."

DR. F. You feel semiconscious.

B. Um-hmm. There's no way to fight. They're still holding my hands down. [Her voice becoming weaker.]

DR. F. Are you still struggling?

B. No.

DR. F. And you're on the ground now and they're kneeling around you?

B. Um-hmm.

DR. F. And what are you aware of physically?

B. The cold stone under me . . . the pressure on my wrists . . . the cold. My dress is all pulled up.

DR. F. Stay very calm and very relaxed. Describe what happens. Relaxing more and more. And now what happens?

B. Well, I guess the blond is first . . . it hurts . . . I'm bleeding.

DR. F. You're bleeding from your vagina?

B. Yes. [Gasping for air.]

DR. F. How do you know that?

B. I can feel it . . . it's warm—and I can feel . . . tearing.

DR. F. Does he do anything else to you?

B. No. He just—he's quick. He gets done really fast.

DR. F. Then what happens?

B. Then the—next guy—the guy without the moustache . . . same thing.

DR. F. Are you experiencing much pain when this is happening?

B. Yes, the second time not as much—or no more, anyways.

DR. F. Do you say anything to them?

B. No. I can hardly even—I—I can hardly tell what's going on.

DR. F. What are you aware of?

B. Just distant sounds . . . they sound far away, but I can feel the pressure—and I can feel the pain—but I can't really see anything. Everything is dark.

DR. F. And now what happens?

B. And the third man . . . and he has a knife—and he cuts me. [Her body shaking.]

DR. F. Where does he cut you?

B. My vagina . . . and my legs.

DR. F. Cuts you before he has intercourse with you?

B. Ah-huh. It hurts a lot and I can feel myself slipping . . . and I guess he rapes me . . . I can't remember . . . [Her voice trailing off.]

DR. F. And now what are you aware of?

B. Nothing.

DR. F. What are you feeling now?

B. Cold.

DR. F. Where do you feel that you are?

B. [Slowly.] Overhead slightly . . . I feel like I'm watching.

DR. F. Are you aware of any sensations, any feelings, any emotions?

B. No, I think I'm dead.

DR. F. What is this then that is doing the observing?

B. My mind?

DR. F. Is that what it feels like?

B. Um-hmm. Feels like it's still me.

DR. F. Do you feel any concern, any worry, any pain?

B. No.

DR. F. What are you aware of feeling?

B. Relieved.

DR. F. And what do you see as you watch?

B. Well, the three of them run away.

DR. F. What do you see as you look down on yourself?

B. A mess . . . of blood. [Distressed.]

DR. F. Stay calm and relaxed. Does this bother you to see this blood and body?

B. In a way, but in a way—it all fits.

DR. F. Tell me what you mean.

B. Well, it bothers me because it means that I've been killed—not very nicely—but I'm relieved, because now I understand why I'm dead, see what I mean?

I asked Elaine to evaluate her life from the spirit plane. She said she felt she had wasted it—that she had really tacitly consented to go with the soldier, to get away from the boredom of her life—that she never developed herself.

Her inner mind revealed the clubbing as the event responsible for her headaches since puberty in this lifetime. It also disclosed the multiple rape as the origin of her sexual dysfunction. As she put it, "I can't relax, I can't enjoy. I don't want anyone touching me like that . . . because the last time they killed me." When I asked her about her years with the soldiers, she admitted she did not have climaxes, that it was "more like a job."

33

Still deeply hypnotized, but back in the present, Becky identified the second rapist as her father in this life. I gave her posthypnotic suggestions to remember only what she could handle emotionally.

Yet, out of the trance, she remembered everything. She shook her head in disbelief as she recalled her discovery about her father. "But he's so perfect. He's the perfect father." After a thoughtful silence, she added that she didn't "hold it against him"—that he was a different person now. She wondered if he had come back as her father this time so he could make up for the past.

The next session after Becky's regression as Elaine was also very revealing. Under hypnosis she could no longer hide a deep-seated hatred of her father. A hatred completely repressed—that triggered migraines, translating her emotional pain into a physical one. She had been paying the price all these years for denying her true feelings. There was a great deal of resistance, even while deeply entranced, to acknowledging both the person she hated and why. This hatred stemmed from the past-life experience of being raped by him. Her inner mind also divulged that her inability to achieve orgasm was due not only to being raped as Elaine, but that a deeply buried part of her remembered her father raping her and this kept her from letting herself go. After we had exposed these feelings she added that something was still missing. Questioned about this, her inner mind slowly showed us a scene of a young girl hacked to death—completely dismembered. She was viewing it from above, from the spirit state. Reconstructing what happened disclosed that in another lifetime she had been imprisoned for being a Catholic. From her cell she jeered at one of her jailors, calling him a homosexual in front of the other prisoners and jailors. Later he crept into her cell, killed her, hacked off her arms and legs, which he cut into pieces in his rage and raped her torso. Her spirit watched this violence, all the while laughing at him. This was the "missing something!"

As we talked after she was out of hypnosis, Becky came to realize that she had always been extremely afraid of her father's anger. She was hypersensitive to it and found herself overreacting. He had never been either physically or verbally abusive to her. She felt very close to him, loved him and wanted to be totally open with him. We decided to ask him to come in with her for her next appointment so that she could share with him all that she now understood about herself. Her biggest concern was that she might hurt him.

The next morning, Saturday, I arranged for them to come in together. Becky's father is a friendly, outgoing man whose intelligent eyes immediately conveyed his sensitivity. Becky, very carefully and straightforwardly, told her father that in a past life he had been one of the men who had raped her as Elaine. She explained that all these years she had been terrified of him because of it—and had carried a deep and subconscious hatred toward him. His eyes were filled with tears as she described the rape scene and how she hadn't wanted to see the men or know who they were. Since Becky had told her family about the details of the regression, he had known about the rape, but not that there was more than one man involved—and especially not that he was one of them.

Tears streaming down his face, he moved over to her and embraced her as she, too, was crying. They continued to sit facing each other, their hands joined. They seemed oblivious of me as they spoke to each other. He said he was filled with remorse that he had hurt her, but there was nothing he could do about that. He vowed to be more controlled with his anger in front of her as he could see—in fact, he had always known—that she was tremendously affected by it, far more than her sisters.

He turned to me, wiping his face with a Kleenex, and said, "Becky and I have always had a special communication. Did she tell you about it?" When I shook my head, he continued, describing a telepathy they shared. He recalled for me several episodes in the past when a strong feeling within him had prompted him to call home, to find that something had just happened to Becky and that she needed him. By now they were smiling, still holding hands. By the time they left all three of us had been deeply moved.

35

Becky was delighted to report to me during our next few bi-monthly sessions that she had been free of migraine headaches. She added, a little sheepishly, "I have had occasional unimportant headaches from time to time which I know are triggered by tension." She was so amazed that, as she put it, "I'm afraid to count the weeks that I've been free of them—they might come back!" She noticed during this period that she was less and less responsive to other people's moods and generally was more relaxed at her job and at school.

She said she responded more each time she and John had sex. With a proud smile, she said, "One time John and I were making love and I felt very dizzy and realized he was getting almost violent with me—violent in terms of the energy and the force behind his thrusting. I remembered the rape scene and told myself to calm down. I did, but naturally I didn't enjoy it anymore that time." She shared her feelings with John and since then they have both enjoyed her increasing responsiveness.

Several weeks later, she called and tearfully told me the migraine problem was not solved. She asked for an earlier appointment, since we were only meeting on a once-a-month basis by then.

As she walked into my office, her face lit up with a big friendly smile. Then, settling herself in her chair, she said, "Here I am back! But there's something my dad figured out that may help us." She pointed out that her headaches always began in the morning in bed, even when she was thirteen. And there was another element of interest—and importance—in our search for understanding. If she went out for breakfast with John, or anyone else, for that matter, she invariably had a migraine that began often before she finished her meal. This convinced her that her headaches were not due to physical factors, but rather, psychological ones. We had missed something in our earlier regressions.

She pushed the chair back into a reclining position, closed her eyes and focused her attention on her breathing.

Deep in trance her finger signals confirmed that the

36

time of day was important because of significant events that had occurred in the morning during the Elaine lifetime. Also, decision-making was of extreme importance as a causative feature. We pinpointed the big decision as her plan to leave her family and go with the soldiers.

I counted her back in time to that event. She lowered her voice conspiratorily:

B. Well, the soldiers will be coming through, that's the rumor, and they'll be bringing some of the women from the towns with . . .

DR. F. They're doing what?

B. They're bringing some women with them and they're taking them.

DR. F. They're bringing women from where?

B. The towns that they're passing through.

DR. F. How do you know that?

B. Someone got word of it in town.

DR. F. Who told you?

B. [Lowering her voice to a whisper.] That man.

DR. F. What man is that?

B. The man who was in front of the shop. He found out.

DR. F. And how did you feel when you heard that?

B. Well, I thought it might be exciting, it might be different . . . it just seemed like the thing to do.

DR. F. Now, where are you when you're hearing this, Elaine?

B. I'm out on the street, shopping. I was just talking to him.

DR. F. And what does he say? Tell me what he says to you.

B. He asks me if I heard about the soldiers. Then he told me that . . . . that there are some girls that are going with them.

DR. F. Did he tell you anything more about what happens to the girls?

B. Well, they live in . . . they get to live in the palace. [Her face brightens up.]

DR. F. Are they paid any money to go?

B. He said they were.

DR. F. How much did he say there were paid?

37

B. Oh, he didn't really say how much, he just said it was—they'd be paid well.

DR. F. What did you think when you heard that?

B. It sounded all right. It sounded like it would be easy and . . . it's a living, you know.

DR. F. What did you think would be involved in going with the soldiers?

B. Oh, I . . . I think I had an inkling that . . . it was basically in the back of my mind that there was sex involved, but I didn't want to . . . that wasn't what I wanted to think about.

DR. F. You heard that while you were shopping on the street?

B. Yeah, he was talking to me.

DR. F. Was he getting the women together or was he just . . .

B. Yeah, I think that he had a stake in it.

DR. F. Did you make any commitment to him at the time?

B. I told him that I wanted to go.

DR. F. You made a spur-of-the-moment decision?

B. Yeah.

DR. F. What time of day is that, that you're making the decision?

B. It's very early in the day.

DR. F. What time would you say? Are the shops open yet?

B. Yeah, it's eight-thirty or nine.

DR. F. Now, how do you feel as you tell him you're going, that you will go. Are you very sure?

B. [In a small voice.] No.

DR. F. A definite, firm commitment?

B. I tell him yes, definitely, but I'm not sure it's quite the thing to do. [Frowning.]

DR. F. And what are the objections that you have in mind?

B. I haven't talked about it with anyone and I think that . . . that thing about sex in the back of my mind is troubling me a little, but then I think it's not that big a deal.

DR. F. Have you ever had sex with anyone, Elaine?

B. No.

DR. F. How old are you now?

B. Sixteen.

DR. F. How do you feel after the man leaves?

B. I'm a bit shaky.

DR. F. Does he tell you where to be at a certain time?

B. He . . . he says to just stay around my home.

DR. F. Did he tell you what day the soldiers would be coming?

B. He said in two days.

DR. F. Then what do you do after you finish talking with him?

B. I get the rest of the food and go home.

DR. F. How do you feel when you go home?

B. Oh, I'm shaky 'cuz I've got a secret and I'm afraid to tell anyone.

DR. F. If you did tell anyone, what do you think would happen?

B. They'd be upset and they would . . . they wouldn't let me go and it's too late because I'm going now whether anyone likes it or not!

DR. F. Why is that?

B. Because I already told him that I would. If I don't go, they'll take me anyway.

DR. F. How do you know that?

B. He told me.

DR. F. That because you said you would go they will take you?

B. Um-hmm.

DR. F. How do you feel when you see your mother?

B. I don't want to look in her eyes. I . . . I'm nervous.

DR. F. Does she notice anything is wrong? Does she pick that up?

B. She just thinks I'm in a funny mood.

DR. F. And then what happens? Move to the next significant event at the count of five. One . . . two . . . . . . three . . . four . . . five.

B. All the soldiers are coming through town . . . and they're . . . I've got my stuff together and I wait till the last minute and I go and tell my parents . . . that I'm leaving.

DR. F. What do they say?

B. Well, they're very upset. They don't understand.

DR. F. What time of day is it?

B. Early.

DR. F. About what time would you say?

B. About nine . . . between nine and ten.

DR. F. Do they try to stop you?

B. Yeah. They try . . . they tell me not to go.

DR. F. How do you feel when they say that?

B. It makes me sad, but I knew that they'd say that.

DR. F. How do you feel as you are getting ready to go . . . when you say goodbye?

B. It's sad but . . . but I decided to do it and so I'm going to.

DR. F. Who was there when you told your parents?

B. No one.

DR. F. Just your mother and father?

B. Um-hmm.

DR. F. Was anyone crying?

B. My mother . . .

DR. F. How does your father react?

B. He's angry.

DR. F. And how do you feel?

B. Umm . . . I'm trying to be stoic, but it's difficult with my mother crying. [Tears forming in her eyes.]

DR. F. And now what happens?

B. They bring me a horse and I get on it.

DR. F. Do they bring the horse to the house?

B. Yeah, well, the house is right on the main street that they're passing through on.

DR. F. Where are you when that happens?

B. I'm coming out of the house to meet them.

DR. F. How do they know it's you?

B. The man that I was talking to in the street is with them. He's showing them where everyone is.

DR. F. And what are the other people in the town doing?

B. They're looking out their windows and discussing what's going on . . .

DR. F. Tell me what you see. A horse is brought to your house?

B. Um-hmm.

40

DR. F. And is anyone leading the horse?

B. Yeah, one of the soldiers.

DR. F. And how do you feel as you get ready to get up onto the horse?

B. I've got to get out of there before I get upset and change my mind . . . and it's too late.

DR. F. What does the soldier say to you?

B. Nothing.

DR. F. Has anyone given you any money?

B. No.

DR. F. How do you feel about that?

B. I haven't thought about that yet.

DR. F. And now what happens? Where are you now?

B. I'm riding out of town.

DR. F. And now move ahead to the next significant event at the count of five. One . . . two . . . three . . . four . . . five and what comes to mind?

B. I'm home again.

DR. F. Tell me what's happening. What are you doing?

B. I'm looking in my house . . .

DR. F. How did you leave the soldiers at the palace? Was it hard for you to do that?

B. No, after a period of time . . . I've been there long enough, so that they didn't really need me that much anymore. They were actually happy to get rid of me . . . because they had younger girls.

DR. F. And so you went to your parents' home. And how did you feel when you were going there?

B. Umm . . . I didn't know whether they'd be glad to see me or not. But there's no one there at all right now.

DR. F. How do you feel when you . . . are you surprised there's no one there?

B. Yeah.

DR. F. What time of day is it?

B. It's early.

DR. F. About what time is it?

B. I suppose it's about eight o'clock.

DR. F. How does the house look? Where do you think your parents are, where your family is?

B. Well, I was looking in the kitchen but they're not there so I go upstairs and there's no one there.

DR. F. What kind of state is the house in?

B. It's not as neat as it normally is.

DR. F. Do you feel calm and relaxed or do you feel . . .

B. No, no. I'm . . . I'm very nervous.

DR. F. Why is that?

B. Because something is obviously wrong.

DR. F. Why do you feel this way?

B. Well, it's early in the day and there's no one out on the street . . . I can't find anyone.

DR. F. Where are you now?

B. I'm out in front of my house.

DR. F. Okay, now just go forward to the next significant event at the count of five and I would like you to get in touch with your thoughts. One . . . two . . . three . . . four . . . five.

B. Well, I'm in my father's shop and I can't find anyone. And I know I did the wrong thing. I shouldn't have gone!

DR. F. Are you blaming yourself in any way?

B. Yes.

DR. F. Tell me about those thoughts.

B. If I hadn't gone I would at least know where they were and I could be with them. I could be helping them if they needed help. I should be with my family. If they've been killed, I want to be dead too.

DR. F. Now move ahead to the next significant event and get in touch with your thoughts. One . . . two . . . three . . . four . . . five. What comes to mind?

B. I'm walking down the street.

DR. F. What are you thinking as you're walking down the street?

B. The same thing over and over.

DR. F. What is that?

B. I should have never gone. Then . . . the men come up behind me . . . push me into the alley . . . hit me on the head.

DR. F. What are you thinking as they're scuffling with you?

42

B. Well, it might as well happen.

DR. F. Why is that?

B. There's nothing else. There's no point in doing anything else.

DR. F. Do you feel that you deserve it?

B. Yes.

DR. F. Why is that?

B. Because I made a stupid mistake and it might have
cost my family their lives.

DR. F. And now what happens?

B. They start raping me!

I quickly brought Becky back to the present since
there was no value to having her go through the trauma
of being raped again. While she was still deeply hypnotized, I questioned her about the relationship between
her migraines and the events she had just recounted.
It became very clear that guilt had been underlying her
headaches all along, that in addition to having had her
head crushed by the club—the incidents we had dealt
with originally. I helped her resolve her guilt by allowing her up-to-date inner mind to review that event in
light of her knowledge and values now.

As Becky came out of the trance, she looked intently
at me and asked, "Do you think that was it?" Nodding,
I replied, "It certainly makes sense, Becky. You felt you
had deserted your family. You felt responsible for their
deaths. Now you realize you weren't responsible, but
that's not how you felt then." "Will that be the end of
the migraines—for good?" she asked with a good deal
of skepticism. I answered, "We'll have to wait and see.
Only time will tell. If there's still something else we've
overlooked then you will certainly know it!" I pointed
out to her that her mind has a way of revealing its
secrets little by little. We saw that, despite her being an
excellent hypnotic subject and a highly motivated patient.

After she left, I thought back over our work together.
I felt deeply impressed by her courage—a courage that
surmounted obstacles of resistance and fear. I see her

as a person who is now able to make monumental changes in the whole fabric of her life.

The last time I saw Becky it had been two months since our last regression. She came in beaming, "Good news. No migraines! Not even one."

CHAPTER THREE

❋

"I'm a Man Wearing a Fur"

Mary Gottschalk, a reporter from the *San Jose Mercury-News*, wrote two articles on my use of past-life regressions with my patients late in 1976. I was soon besieged with calls from many people wanting to explore their past lives. Some had particular problems they were sure came from the distant past, but most just wanted to know who they had been before. Caren, my secretary, schedules nonpatient past-life regressions on Saturdays. These appointments hold special interest for me because in two hours I meet at least two people—the person as he or she exists now and a very different individual, often of the opposite sex, from a bygone era. On a Saturday in mid-January of 1977, I met two who impressed me deeply.

Jackie is a very pretty, petite young woman in her late twenties. Her dark, twinkling eyes match her short, curly black hair. She came armed with a mental list of what she planned to tell me. I had the feeling she wanted to make full use of every minute. She was particularly interested in understanding her turbulent relationship with her husband, whom she had remarried after many separations and reunions. She guessed they might have had past-life experiences that could throw light on their frantic on-again, off-again merry-go-round life. Just in case we might run into no past-life links or head-on into insurmountable resistance in this area, I asked her what else was of interest. She said that ever since her teens she had had very active, exciting and vivid dreams of being a Mohican Indian—of killing many people. She/he had a "fantastic" body, with long, strong legs, and wore only a loin cloth. Somehow the killing was done

45

with a purpose—to right a wrong. But part of her dreaming self could not handle the taking of human life. She added that she remembered a *déjà vu* experience that happened when she was ten, a particularly unhappy period in her childhood. She recalled looking out over the Bay Area from a bluff and "knowing" that she had been there before, or in some other similar place, doing the same thing. She shuddered and said, "It was an *eerie* feeling." She brought herself back to the topic of the regression and decided she wanted to explore the origins of her "multi-talents." She is a bookkeeper. In her spare time she paints and plays the organ. Recently she ran an art gallery. But somehow she feels "bottled up," as though she is not really finding an outlet for her creativity.

I began the hypnotic induction. Her eyelids started to flutter the moment she closed them. Her breathing and the pulse in her neck slowed down immediately. Within seconds I recognized that she was an excellent subject. But we soon ran head-first into a brick wall of resistance. Her inner mind stubbornly refused to deal with her relationship with her husband. For a tantalizing half-hour she reported seeing only fleeting colors and being aware of bodily sensations. No images! No thoughts! I decided to tackle another area. I asked her inner mind to take her to an event in a lifetime that would help her understand why she felt bottled up and could not express her creativity.

At the count of ten, her voice became much lower and she slowly and laboriously told her story:

J. [Mumbling, apparently puzzled.] This can't be what I'm seeing.
DR. F. What are you seeing?
J. [Slowly.] Cave walls. It's crude . . . there's no tools . . . it's still so far back.
DR. F. Tell me what you're feeling.
J. . . . I'm alone.
DR. F. What are you doing?
J. Just standing.
DR. F. Where are you?

J. On a cliff . . . near a cave . . . Humph! I'm a man wearing a . . . fur.

DR. F. What is the fur like?

J. Heavy—and thick.

DR. F. Tell me about yourself.

J. I'm not straight—I'm crooked . . . but not crooked . . . I'm . . . Humph! . . . I'm looking for something? I'm looking out over something. [Voice full of astonishment.]

DR. F. Are you very high up?

J. Up . . . up above a valley . . . I'm scroungy . . . and it's deserty, it's not in the mountains and trees— it's dry. The cave is mine . . . I'm looking for something and I don't see it . . . I'm waiting.

DR. F. Get in touch with how you feel and get in touch with who you are—whether you have other people who belong with you.

J. There's people somewhere, but they're not there . . . I have paintings in my cave and I'm protecting them.

DR. F. Who did them.

J. [Proudly.] They're mine.

DR. F. How did you do them?

J. Rock, bits of rock . . . it's hard—and long—and they're mine.

DR. F. How did you actually do those paintings?

J. With my hands.

DR. F. What else did you use?

J. No tools—there was nothing.

DR. F. What did you use for paints?

J. I had none . . . I had none. Used just a rock.

DR. F. You used a rock to draw your designs?

J. On the wall, I scraped . . . I was trying to say something—and I'm looking for someone and guarding them, but I want someone—to see what I have to say. I have no speech. I have no way of speaking.

DR. F. Do others around you have ways of speaking?

J. I don't know. There's no one here but me.

DR. F. Do you have a family?

J. I don't remember.

DR. F. What is it that you're saying in those drawings— those paintings?

47

J. It's a whole wall. It's life . . . and animals. There always has to be animals. [Matter-of-factly.]

DR. F. Why is that?

J. They're part of everything.

DR. F. What kind of animals are there?

J. They're herds—they're moving. There's lots of animals.

DR. F. Now what are you experiencing?

J. [Laughs.] I'm back and forth between my conscious—and my vision.

DR. F. Just let yourself slip into the vision . . . and tell me about the animals. What kind of animals did you paint?

J. Hmm . . . the herd animals. Big ones and little ones—and they're moving—and they move on my wall as I've seen them.

DR. F. What else have you drawn on your wall?

J. [Pause.] I have a club with a rock.

DR. F. Are the rock and the club joined in some way?

J. Leather. They're crossed and crisscrossed. I made that—I made it myself.

DR. F. What do you use it for?

J. I don't like to think. [Shaking her head.]

DR. F. What do you use it for?

J. Protect.

DR. F. Whom do you protect or what do you protect yourself from?

J. I don't see them, but I'm looking.

DR. F. What are you looking for?

J. It's a big valley—and the cave is very high. It's a jumble of rocks, dry rocks, round rocks—and I'm standing, looking . . . I'm alone here.

DR. F. Where were you before you came to the cave?

J. [Evasively.] I'm cast out.

DR. F. Tell me more.

J. I'm cast out.

DR. F. From?

J. Everything. [Said with amazement.]

DR. F. How did that happen?

J. I'm strange and I'm different. Some things are not right with me.

DR. F. In what way are you strange and different?

J. I know things . . . I know things.

DR. F. Can you tell me more about that?

J. I'm here. I am so strange. [Laughs.]

DR. F. How do you feel you're strange?

J. I'm crossing back . . . I'm so . . . older.

DR. F. Describe yourself.

J. I'm hairy—not all over my body, but my hair is matted and ugly . . . and it's not dark hair . . . [Sighs.] . . . but my eyes don't belong . . . I know more than the others.

DR. F. Do you look like the others?

J. I can't remember them.

DR. F. Was that a long time ago?

J. It must have been because I'm so lonely.

DR. F. In what way do your eyes not belong?

J. My eyes aren't at the . . . hmm . . . my eyes know more than the man that I'm in—but I'm in this man—and this is all there is.

DR. F. And you're trying to communicate to others . . .

J. But I couldn't communicate . . .

DR. F. Why is that?

J. They didn't understand.

DR. F. Were you speaking the same language that they spoke?

J. I could only communicate with my hands.

DR. F. Why is that?

J. I don't know if I had speech or not.

DR. F. How did you communicate with your hands?

J. I drew . . . drew pictures.

DR. F. Did the others draw pictures too?

J. No!

DR. F. How did they communicate?

J. They're different. I'm different—from them.

DR. F. Tell me more about this.

J. They're different. They're . . . they don't understand. They're struggling . . . [Deep, hopeless sigh.] . . . they don't live in the cave. They live in the valley.

DR. F. When you say you know things, what do you mean? Can you tell me more about that?

49

J. I know . . . hmm . . . I'm to teach them—and I can't teach them. They're at another . . . they're somewhere else and I can't reach them, and they won't learn, and I use my pictures . . . they're children. I'm older . . . they're children . . . in this life . . . I know more—and I can't teach them because they won't accept me.

DR. F. When you say "children," do you mean that they're actually grown people, but they are children in terms of their development?

J. They're children, yes.

DR. F. What is it that you have to teach them?

J. Everything. Everything . . . everything. They have to know. [Gestures with a broad sweep of her hands.]

DR. F. Tell me some of these things.

J. Life . . . they have to know about life.

DR. F. What is it about life that you'd like to teach them?

J. To raise them—to get them out of where they're at. They're living—horribly—and I'm no better, but I'm different . . . than they. I have blue eyes . . . I have blue eyes, that's what's different! They're all dark. And my eyes . . . my eyes are more . . . they're bright—bright eyes. They're dark and black—and black hair and greasy and naked, and I'm not naked . . . and where did I come from?

DR. F. At the count of three you'll know where you came from. One . . . two . . . three.

J. Goth? . . . Goth.

DR. F. How did you come from Goth? [Could he have been among those Goths involved in a social revolution around the fourth century A.D. who migrated to Africa?]

J. I traveled . . . a long way.

DR. F. How did you travel?

J. There was a boat, there was a boat—a funny boat.

DR. F. In what way was it funny?

J. There was a beach and it was hot—but it was only me. There's no one with me . . . My head! [Groans.]

DR. F. Just go on.

J. I wasn't as ugly as at the cave. I was not as worn—I was stronger . . . was different there. But this is strange, dry land—and hot . . . I don't remember traveling—but I must have traveled—but I don't remember the route. Two mountains and a valley . . . and the people . . . black hair, black and thick . . . and they scurry around. They're smaller than I am. I'm tall and big . . . there's a dog . . . there's a dog. There's children, babies . . . I'm tired. [Sounding exhausted.]

DR. F. How long have you been alone?

J. . . . Forever.

DR. F. What do you mean?

J. I'm singular.

DR. F. Can you tell me more?

J. There is no one . . . I can remember, except these people—and myself—and I know and I'm different.

DR. F. Were there others like you long ago in another place, another time?

J. They got lost. They didn't . . . they got lost. They weren't on the ship.

DR. F. Are you on the ship by yourself?

J. I am alone . . . I am alone. They aren't with me.

DR. F. And what happened to them?

J. Now there's a battle . . . How did I? . . . There is a battle, somewhere—somewhere.

DR. F. It will become clearer and clearer to you and you will remember.

J. There's swords—and axes—and round guards . . . and there's fighting, everybody's close together fighting, fighting . . . killing.

DR. F. Are there many people doing this? About how many?

J. It's all men—all fighting—small. It's not big, but just my men.

DR. F. Are they fighting each other, is that it?

J. No. Others like us . . . and I don't know why.

DR. F. You will remember why at the count of three. One . . . two . . . three.

J. Village—and there's hate . . . I hate. [Sounding shocked.]

DR. F. Why is that?

J. I feel it. I don't understand it.

DR. F. It will become very clear to you at the count of three. One . . . two . . .three.

J. I don't understand. [Long pause.]

DR. F. What do they call you?

J. I'm Bright-Eyes! [Voice becoming enthusiastic.]

DR. F. They call you Bright-Eyes?

J. Bright-Eyes.

DR. F. Who calls you that? . . . Who calls you Bright-Eyes?

J. My people, but not my new people.

DR. F. What do your new people call you?

J. They can't speak. They don't speak—the way I speak.

DR. F. How do they speak?

J. Oh, it's gibberish. [Disdainfully.] . . . I don't understand, and they don't understand me.

DR. F. You said that you had no speech. Did something happen to you?

J. I think my throat was cut. Something was cut.

DR. F. It will become very clear to you at the count of three. One . . . two . . . three.

J. Two—the tongue and the cords, my cords.

DR. F. Who did that to you?

J. It happened before I sailed.

DR. F. How?

J. Punishment for something. Punishment . . . I didn't want to fight . . . I wouldn't fight. [With determination.] I was accepted by my people—but still an outsider, because I wouldn't fight. I watched the fight . . . I had a belt. I *made* the belt! It was leather—and it crossed my shoulders in the fur—but I lost it. At the cave I just have the fur.

DR. F. What's happening now?

J. . . . Unsuccessful.

DR. F. Unsuccessful? Can you tell me what you mean by that?

J. I've lost my people, or been sent away . . . and I
. . . found new people . . . and I'm alone.

DR. F. Why were you sent away?

J. Fighting . . . fighting . . . I wouldn't.

DR. F. Now who sent you away?

J. All the people.

DR. F. Were they your people who sent you away?

J. Yes.

DR. F. Now, I'd like you to move to the last day of your
life at the count of five. Become aware of what happens. One . . . two . . . three . . . four . . . five.

J. Ahh . . . they turned. I waited alone . . . to draw
them pictures, to show them things . . . and I lived
in the cave . . . and they threw rocks at me. They
wouldn't accept. I was strange to them . . . I'm under rocks.

DR. F. Have you died?

J. I knew I was going to. Was really . . .

DR. F. Just experience what happens the moment after
your death, become aware of how you feel, what's
going on.

J. [Silence.]

DR. F. All right now, I'd like you to go to a few moments
before your death and become aware of what's happening. They're throwing stones and rocks at you?

J. They surrounded me.

DR. F. I'd like you to describe what's happening.

J. I had a club . . . but I couldn't use it.

DR. F. Why couldn't you use your club? Were there too
many of them?

J. There were lots of them . . . [Long, drawn-out
sigh.] . . . But I couldn't . . . couldn't hit them.

DR. F. Why is that?

J. They don't know what they're doing—I would know
what I am doing.

DR. F. What are they doing to you?

J. They're all throwing rocks—in front of my cave—at
me. [Said in a soft, removed voice.]

DR. F. Where are you?

J. On the ledge.

53

DR. F. And where are they?

J. They're gone now . . . and I'm under rocks.

DR. F. I'd like you to go to the moment of your death and become aware of where you were hit.

J. . . . All over.

DR. F. Were you hit on the head?

J. From behind, up above . . .

DR. F. And how did it feel?

J. There wasn't pain—there was numbness.

DR. F. And then what happened?

J. There were more—and more, but I don't feel them anymore. I don't . . . it's only a body.

DR. F. Where are you?

J. In a . . . in a pile . . . on a ledge and they keep throwing rocks until they pile . . . all over me.

DR. F. Are you in your body when this is happening?

J. Yes.

DR. F. And you don't feel any more rocks?

J. No pain.

DR. F. What are you aware of?

J. How sad! [Short laugh.]

DR. F. What do you mean?

J. Poor people . . . I failed—I failed.

DR. F. Is there something that you could have done to keep yourself from failing?

J. I was limited. My tools were limited.

After she came out of the trance, Jackie blinked and stared at me disbelievingly. She slowly said that she was still reeling from being overwhelmed by pity, sadness and the feeling of frustration and failure. "It was so real," she murmured. She added, shaking her head, "I had so many pictures in my mind—a lot of things I saw I couldn't describe." She said that at first she had had to strain—the memories were from so long ago. She dropped into deep thought and finally said, "I will have a lot to mull over in the next days and weeks."

Remembering how hard she had labored to produce an answer to my questions, I asked her if she had trouble communicating verbally in this lifetime. Tears welled in her eyes as she nodded her head. She confessed she found it very hard to express herself verbally—and was frequently not "heard," especially by those close to her.

As she paused at the door, about to leave, she frowned and told me she was disappointed she had not been able to get back to a lifetime with her husband. After the door closed behind her, I wondered if she realized what a gem she had uncovered! What a sensitive, highly evolved and compassionate man Bright-Eyes had been. I am so glad to have known him.

❖

CHAPTER FOUR

"I Know What's Behind That Door!"

The tiny blue light on the wall signaled that my new patient had arrived for her first appointment—thirty-five minutes late! "How *dumb* of me! I thought it was for eleven, not ten. I'm never late—in fact, I'm always early for appointments." Her face was red, her voice strained. Through my mind flashed a thought—what colossal resistance! This will be uphill all the way!

Elizabeth, an overweight woman in her mid-thirties, wore a sad, hangdog expression. Her large, morose brown eyes were underlined with deep, dark circles. Her dress was casual; she had squeezed her twenty extra pounds into jeans two sizes too small. A dark and rather dreary T-shirt and Adidas tennis shoes completed the careless picture. Her close-cropped dark hair, flecked with gray, and lack of any make-up suggested to me that this woman did not think much of herself.

I wondered if she were afraid to sit with her back to the door, since she had declined my original suggestion to sit in the usual patient chair, the recliner.

Although we could only spend a short time together that first session, Elizabeth was able to communicate to me her imperative and desperate need for help. As she put it, "It's just *got* to work!" She eased into specifics by declaring that weight control was her main concern. "I've been fat all my life. Even when I was in the third grade, I looked like a pumpkin with a ball on top." She outlined the shape with her hands. We both had to laugh. (There was lightness there—a good sign.) Originally two hundred and fifteen pounds, she battled her fat for the past two years until she lost eighty-five pounds. But now the pounds, and inches, were starting to steal back on. Chris, her husband, preferred that she be slim, which compounded the problem. She described a rather common and compulsive eating pattern—waking up in the morning with a "This is it!" attitude, yet unable to resist eating two peanut-butter-and-jelly sandwiches with a huge glass of milk for lunch, followed by remorse for being "weak." In those rare moments when she thought she might feel good about herself, she had to do something to counteract her positive feelings. "It's defeating! I'm not hungry, why eat it? But another part of me says, 'Shut up and eat it!' " So, if she lost a few pounds, she would be sure to "binge" or give in to an irresistible hot fudge sundae. Then dieting would become a form of punishment for her and she would feel better. A pernicious and vicious cycle! And a pattern that surfaced in other areas of her life—spending money, involving herself in projects, exercising.

Covering her mouth with her hands, as though to hide the words—and thoughts—she edged with hesitance and pain into her real problems. Ones that she had struggled with all her life. With an exasperated look, she told of being beset by fears—of heights, snakes, lizards, spiders, of "everything!" To add to the burden, she had been immobilized for years by profound depressions. "I live on antidepressants. I have been morose as long as I can remember," she mumbled. "I've felt guilty all my life . . . I don't know what I'm guilty of. So I find things!" She clenched her fists, as she literally spat out all the ways she immolated herself. Even coming for help was a cause for self-flagellation. To have to spend so much money on herself! As she recounted her past, she sketched a portrait of extreme periodic depressions. Several years ago, she was drawn into a very deep depression that lasted for three years. During these years she would just sit for hours on end—and the other hours she read in bed. Doing the smallest chore was a major undertaking that exhausted her. She was slipping hopelessly into the same pattern now and it scared her. "It's a constant battle," she sighed. During the depression she was describing she recalled that she cried a great deal. At that time her main fear was that she would kill herself in her sleep. Her husband would periodically hide all the knives and razor blades. She had never made an overt attempt to destroy herself, but in many not so subtle ways she tried to force her life to end prematurely. She had an ulcer that hemorrhaged for months. When she recovered from that, she developed another serious disease, thyroiditis, and then another—and another.

Through the years she had seen psychiatrists who prescribed antidepressants and tranquilizers. There were therapists who "just would not talk. It was one long, horrendous experience! One even stopped all my medication, even antidepressants. And, still he wouldn't talk to me—except to say 'Hmmm.' " More than once her physicians had recommended immediate institutionalization. She refused. With a desperate look, she admitted, "I don't know *why* I was so afraid to go to the hospital. I even made my husband sign a statement that he would never—no matter how bad off I was—allow them to commit me." Before she came for treatment to me, her husband asked her to check into the psychiatric wing of a local hospital. Just for one day! "Our insurance company would have paid eighty percent of the fee. I could *not* stand the thought of even twenty-four hours there." Finished with her "confession," she stopped talking and looked at me pleadingly.

I asked her why she had decided to see me. She replied immediately, "I read in the paper about your work. Somehow I know these anxieties have been carried over from past lives. There's nothing in this life that could cause all this *grief*."

The next time we met, Elizabeth spelled out what "these anxieties" were. She began by confessing that the week before she had felt a "great wave of guilt" because she was late for her appointment. "I can't allow myself to make a mistake." Besides guilt, *any* mistake, no matter how small, generated anxiety. Shuddering, she went on to say she couldn't stand to see anything violent or destructive. "Horror and abuse and misuse of people scares me." She was revolted by the sight of the slightest amount of blood. If one of her three children were injured and bleeding, even from a minor scratch, she would "freak out." She could feel their pain. She would hurt inside. She couldn't watch her children being born, even though she opted for natural childbirths. Because of the blood, she insisted that the nurse cover the mirror with a towel. She carefully selected nonviolent movies. She scanned reviews and advertisements to make sure she could tolerate them. She checked with friends before venturing to a show. Even that didn't always work for her. She had to rush out many times, on the verge of throwing up. "I even have to read mysteries little by little," she explained. "I saw an operation on TV and I could *feel* the patient's pain. And I get so sentimental. I cry over dumb shows."

But by far the most crippling of all her anxieties was a terror of coming home and finding her three children harmed. Now that they were all teenagers and beyond the age of needing a babysitter, she felt even more anxious. Each outing was a painful occasion. Returning home from the few she permitted herself, she insisted her husband check on the children. She would remain "really uptight and scared" in their car. Only until he could reassure her that they were fine could she bring herself to go in, too. When I questioned her more closely about what she imagined might have happened, she bit her hand and grimaced. "Somebody will break into the house—kill the children at night. It's always with a knife. Always awful!" Her overconcern for her children permeated all corners of their lives. She worried if they were near a railing. She worried if one was more than ten minutes late returning home. She worried about their getting hurt, lost, not doing well, not having friends—and on and on. "I'm afraid the kids will draw knives. I just don't want them to fight. But I can't make them understand." She wrung her hands. "And the perpetual guilt! I *can't* say no to them."

Before the session ended, I tried to teach Elizabeth self-hypnosis. I suggested she close her eyes and concentrate on her breathing. Instead, she sat bolt upright. With her eyes wide open she said, "I'm really worried about finding out. Maybe I'm *right* to be guilty—

59

something that can't be changed. What if I killed someone in a previous life? But I couldn't. It's not my basic personality." Then, with a pleading voice, "Maybe it's better left alone." I discussed some other relevant cases with her. I showed her how others, through understanding—both intellectually and at a gut level—overcame their symptoms and problems. Finally, she slowly sank against the back of the chair, closed her eyes and said, sounding troubled, "Okay, I'm ready." I started again, but within a minute her eyes sprang open. "I feel frightened." She suggested that she might relax better on the floor. "Why don't we try that, then?" I said. So she eased her troubled body to the floor. "Is that better?" I asked. "I think so," she said. I gave her calming suggestions, asking her to close her eyes as I talked to her. The muscles of her face softened. Her hands relaxed. Her breathing became deeper and more regular. The pulse that had been visibly racing in her neck also quieted down. After progressively relaxing her body, she awakened quickly to my suggestions. She smiled. "That felt good!" I asked her to listen to the tape I recorded for her twice daily. Then we set up her appointment for the next week.

When she returned, she began the session by announcing that the tape didn't help. She would get to a certain point, beginning really to relax—then snap out of it. She couldn't trust *herself*. She might find out something. Then it hit her—something that had been there for years. "I can't be happy. I can't let go. I'm afraid of what might be there." She couldn't let her guard down because she must keep herself from finding out. Again I was very aware that in helping her face her inner self, I had my work cut out for me.

Wondering to what degree she hid from herself, I asked her whether she dreamed. "No dreams." However, there was a recurring nightmare, one she described as "progressive," because it altered somewhat with each dream. When she was growing up she wanted two things: a husband and a Victorian house. After she was married, she would occasionally dream that:

60

> We buy a beautiful old house. We work on it. It
> becomes even more beautiful. Gradually, a little
> more with each dream, I see the interior. It's very
> charming with lots of wood. But I never see the
> upstairs.

She added that when she became aware that she had
not seen the upstairs, she slipped into her first "horrible
depression." Her voice trembled as she described the
first time, many years ago, that she forced herself up
the stairs.

> It was the most terrifying night of my life—the ef-
> fort it took to climb those stairs! The house
> started deteriorating. I started forcing myself to go
> upstairs. There were absolute terrors in each room.
> I would find monsters, snakes, spiders, terrible
> things I couldn't handle in those rooms. And they
> were *filthy*. I would clean each one up only to
> have it get messed up again. But with a great deal
> of effort, it would finally stay clean. Then the
> house became happy.

At this point, three years later, her depression lifted.
(This corroborated my unspoken assumption that the
house symbolized her mind.) She then recalled a very
frightening experience that happened at about the same
time. Feeling energetic enough to get out of the house at
last, she took a tour of old houses and visited a farmhouse. She was about to enter one room, when she
found herself temporarily paralyzed with fear. "I *knew*
that if I had crossed that threshold, I would not get
home alive. There was tragedy in that room. I couldn't
stay in that house . . . I ran out, shaking—until I got
home." She trembled even as she was recalling the incident. I spent a few minutes quieting her.

She then reported that on the night before our appointment, she had experienced the recurring nightmare. "But this time, there is one more room up
there—an attic room. I *cannot* bring myself to even
imagine what's there!"

61

I saw Elizabeth once a week for several months. During this time, she continued the pattern of starting the session sitting in the chair facing the door but lying on the floor when we used hypnosis. Despite her fears, she always kept her appointments—usually coming half an hour early. She practiced with the tape at least once each day despite great inner resistance. She relaxed more and more with her self-hypnosis as she learned to trust me—and especially herself.

As we met week after week, I learned a great deal more about her. She has an intimate and affectionate relationship with her very supportive husband. "We love each other and we *like* each other. We've had a problem with sex for years, because of the depression. I can't let go. What if I did and something happened to the kids. I'm waiting and listening all the time. We have learned to live with it. We adjusted to it this way, and yet it's a disappointment for both of us. But I can't allow myself to let go." She told about one problem she had solved years ago. "My one big fear then was that he would leave. I used to be so worried about it all the time. He finally drummed into my head that he would never leave me—never, for any reason. He convinced me there was no reason to feel that way. Now it's not a big fear. But I still have an awful fear of his being away—maybe someone will break in. I'm forever checking the locks and the windows. It's really bad at night." Apart from their sexual problem and her anxiety when he is away, they seemed to have a truly loving relationship.

Her three children, Betsy, Mark and Judy, are "good kids," despite the usual teenage dramas. Her oldest daughter, Betsy, has had problems off and on through the years. "She's pretty bossy with the others—the little mother. They don't like it." Elizabeth worried about Betsy. "Sometimes she gets pretty anxious and down. I hope she isn't going to have the same problems I have."

She continued to complain about her weight, saying that she couldn't even fit in her jeans and they were her daily "uniform." (She still came each week in her outfit

62

of jeans and a T-shirt.) I asked her to be patient about her weight. We needed to deal with the underlying causes. I emphasized that she was under enough stress without trying to diet. She was quick to agree.

One week she finally was able to establish finger signals! I then questioned her inner mind. But I ran into a not unexpected wall of resistance. Most of my questions were answered with her "I don't want to answer" finger. Three sessions later her subconscious mind divulged that her problems originated in previous lives. I gave her posthypnotic suggestions to be prepared the next time to deal with the events that were causing her psychic pain.

She came in the following week, dropped in the chair and started to cry. Tears running down her cheeks, she said she didn't want to talk about herself this week. "Something has come up. It's Betsy." She related incidents from the past two weeks or so that indicated that Betsy needed immediate psychological help. It sounded to me as if the girl were severely depressed herself. I recommended an excellent female therapist for her. I felt, but did not share the feeling with Elizabeth, that Betsy was somehow resonating to the upheaval her mother was experiencing as a result of our work. I also sensed that this was a timely red herring. We had a few minutes left, so I asked Elizabeth to let me give her some hypnotic suggestions that would help her for our next meeting. She consented and lay down on the floor. After the trance was induced, I gave her inner mind strong, repeated suggestions to prepare her at a subconscious level "to be ready to look at the events that are responsible for your problems."

Apparently my suggestions scared her away! She canceled her next appointment the day before she was due, flourishing a "bad cold."

But the next week, she came, as usual a half-hour early. As I walked out to get her, I wondered if this would be it. Would she be able to regress to a past life? She came in looking a little tense. We spent a few minutes talking about her daughter. She seemed to be feeling better already and liked her therapist. Finally, Elizabeth got enough off her chest to relax. I put her in a trance and she attempted to go back to the lifetime responsible for her fears. She slowly received a few vague impressions. Then she felt a deep sadness welling up within her. She spontaneously brought herself completely out of the trance. "I don't think I can do it. There's something *very* frightening there." I asked her to relax and gave her more suggestions to prepare herself, hoping they would filter down to her subconscious mind.

The following two weeks she complained that the antidepressants weren't helping. She felt "a deep, deep sadness." She woke up each morning feeling distraught and distressed. She was not as relaxed with the tapes as she was before. And she was getting "fatter and fatter." She was beginning to question the feasibility of continuing. I explained that all of this was a sign we were getting close to important material.

Fortunately, she was finally able to visualize much more and pieced together vignettes of an extremely sad childhood and early married life as a woman living in the eighteen hundreds in Europe. As had been her custom, she lay on the floor for the hypnotic work. This time, after the induction, when she was deeply relaxed, she asked to sit in the reclining chair (with her back to the door!). She got up, walked to the chair, flopped down into it and within a few seconds picked up the threads from the past few weeks and was reliving the rest of that lifetime in the eighteen hundreds. It was so staggeringly traumatic it took us an hour and fifteen minutes to get through it. During most of it, she wept and sobbed hysterically—unable to continue at times. In it, as the only responsible adult in an orphanage, she had to stand by helplessly and watch her thirty young charges—all her beloved little boys and girls—burn excruciatingly to death. She was alone at the time. Her husband was out of town on business. She couldn't speak the language of the country she was in—India— so she couldn't go for help. After the regression she was completely exhausted. I was puzzled. It didn't completely fit the picture of her symptoms. I was remembering the fear she had for her own children. The regression explained the guilt she had carried all her life, and her fear of having her husband away from her. But I kept going back in my mind to the picture of her sitting in the car while her husband went in to make sure her children were alive. I was in suspense until the following week.

"I was exhausted for three days. But I don't really feel any better. In fact, I was generally down and depressed all week." I knew that we had more work to do. And work we did. She went back to a lifetime as a sea captain. Another as a first mate. Still another as a sea captain's much-neglected wife. They were all interesting lives and each in some way had affected her current life. But she as yet hadn't achieved the relief she sought. During this period of her therapy the strain was too much for her and she dropped out of college. (She had been taking a few anthropology courses.) "I had three problems: myself, Betsy and school. One *had* to go." She felt disgusted with herself. "To make matters worse, I'm eating and eating and gaining weight. It feels futile. I feel very pessimistic." Off and on she could not stand listening to the tape.

Then, one week, fourteen sessions after our first meeting she came in with a smile. She announced that she was feeling good. She had even discontinued her antidepressants. She had been able to tolerate listening to the tape three times a day for the past week. "Sometimes when I listen to it now, all of a sudden I am so relaxed, I almost fall asleep." Even her husband had commented to her that she seemed much more relaxed and self-confident. (So the regressions were beginning to pay off after all.) Her eyes lit up as she started to tell me about a dream she had the night before. With an apologetic look, she said, "It has nothing to do with my problems. But since I never dream, except for that nightmare, I thought you would like to hear it." I asked her to describe the dream, recorded here verbatim:

It was about a house. Not the one I told you about before. It started off as my grandmother's house and then became ours, the one we live in. A person came over to visit. We were watching color TV which is strange, because our set is black and white. There was a hidden part to the house. In fact, it was almost another whole house. Walking through a closet, I went to look at it. It could have been arranged so beautifully. There were lovely antiques and mementos and neat stuff. It was not terrifying. I wanted to show it so bad to the friend. I really liked this part. But I had never gotten around to it. I imagined what it could look like if we fixed it up. It needs paint, time, money and muscle. I can't do it myself. It could be the loveliest part of the whole house. Then the guest came and I wanted so hard to show them—the guest was a couple, and yet one person. That's weird. Everytime I started to mention it, other things came up. I wanted them to know about the room. Even though we had lived there for some time, I had never shown anyone this room. Finally they left and I realized I hadn't gotten to show it to them. I was *so* disappointed.

After relating the dream, she added, "It would be so beautiful if I could only get someone to help me put it right. It's like that terrifying upstairs attic room . . . but it's not the same. I wish I could finish that dream."

I sensed that the "someone" was me and that she was asking for help in solving the final riddle. Following that hunch, I suggested she finish the dream under hypnosis. I asked her to close her eyes, concentrate on her breathing and relax. In seconds, not very deep in trance at all, she said, "The word 'murder' just flashed through my mind. I'm not sure whether it was conscious or not." Wringing her hands she said, "red, knife, curls, little girl's nightie, a farm," and added, " 'party' came to mind." I thought she was easing into a past life. I hadn't given her any suggestions to go back in time—did not count her back. She had just gotten there by herself. This was special—and important! I asked her where she was.

E. My kitchen . . . it's in a small farmhouse.

DR. F. What's happening?

E. I just—just finished dinner and, ah . . . we're bathing the kids and—it's taking us such a long time! [Impatiently.]

DR. F. It seems to be taking a long time?

E. Um-hmm. She just keeps finding things, "Wash their hair again, wash their ears again, wash the" . . . just ah . . . she's upset and nervous and she keeps finding things to go over. [Becoming even more annoyed.]

DR. F. How do you feel about that?

E. I just want to get it done!

DR. F. Who is there?

E. My sister-in-law and the three kids . . . and the cat.

DR. F. How old are the children?

E. The oldest is ten . . . and a girl, six . . . and the baby. She's a girl. The oldest is a boy.

DR. F. What is your name?

E. Sarah? . . . Yes, Sarah.

DR. F. What are you doing now?

E. I'm getting ready to go somewhere . . . umm . . . and ah . . . *she* doesn't want to go.

DR. F. She doesn't want to go?

E. That's why—maybe that's why there's tension. Ah . . . it's angry in here and we've had a fight or something and that's—I'm just too angry to think . . . just . . . she's being foolish and she's being silly and . . . and ah . . . I'm just fed up with her. She just sits around and whines and complains and she never goes anywhere. She never does anything and . . . and ah . . . she doesn't want me to do anything, either.

DR. F. Doesn't want you to go out, is that it?

E. Um-hmm.

DR. F. Where is her husband?

E. He doesn't work at home. He works away from home.

DR. F. What does he do?

E. He works on a—on a neighboring farm, only it isn't the next door farm. It is a ways away and ah . . .

67

we have a small place and in order to earn money he hires out . . . it is harvest time and he hired out.

DR. F. Is their marriage happy?

E. It isn't even a relationship. They are just married.

DR. F. What is the occasion tonight?

E. There's just a party . . . wait a minute, it's not just a party, what is it?

DR. F. At the count of three you will know. One . . . two . . . three and what comes to mind?

E. [Smiling.] Oh! Friends of ours got married and they're home from their honeymoon and they're moving into their new house and . . . and we've been invited . . . and they said to bring the kids, that the kids could sleep upstairs . . . and they would like us both to come.

DR. F. Will there be other people at the party?

E. Yeah. It's just a . . . it's a small town and everyone knows everyone and . . . other kids will be there and they just put mattresses on the floor upstairs and all the kids will sleep there. And she doesn't want to go. [With sarcasm.] But yet she says she never goes anywhere.

DR. F. How does she feel about your going?

E. Well, she says she doesn't want me to go, but she just ah . . . she never wants me to go. [Very irritated.] She's always lonely . . . unhappy and depressed. She said she had a rough day and she just doesn't want to be there alone.

DR. F. Is there anybody that you want to see at the party? Anyone that you're looking forward to seeing?

E. [She seems to be searching her mind.]

DR. F. At the count of three. One . . . two . . . three.

E. No. The name David comes, but that's ah . . . there's no one in particular, no.

DR. F. Just move ahead a few moments in time and see what you wear and how you prepare yourself for the party at the count of three. One . . . two . . . three and what comes to mind?

E. Oh, dear. [Biting her lip.]

DR. F. What's the matter? Is something wrong?

E. [Silence.]

DR. F. Do you want to tell me?

E. [Shakes her head no.]

DR. F. Why is that? You're shaking your head no. You can tell me. I'm a doctor. I'm used to hearing things. Just feel free to talk about it.

E. [Deep sigh]

DR. F. I'm going to count from one to five and at the count of five you will find it much, much easier to tell me about it. One . . . two . . . three . . . four . . . five.

E. Ohhh . . . I just had a bad feeling. . . it'll go away. It's just a bad feeling.

DR. F. Where are you right now?

E. I'm climbing the stairs and I'm going into my room . . . and I, ah . . . I just—it's just a funny feeling, that's all . . . that's . . . you know how you get funny feelings . . . I just don't think I should go . . . I just don't think I should go.

DR. F. When you say "funny feeling," what does it mean? Does it mean that you have some thoughts or . . .

E. [Interrupting.] Yeah.

DR. F. Tell me about it.

E. Oh . . .

DR. F. What came to mind?

E. Well, when I walked up the stairs to my room . . . and I was going to open the door . . . I just got this *horrible* feeling of fear and . . . and . . . and I shouldn't go. [Shaking her head repeatedly.] I—I shouldn't go . . . and it—I can't find any reason why I shouldn't go.

DR. F. Do you have those feelings often?

E. Not really, no. No. Hmmm . . .

DR. F. You didn't want to tell me about that feeling?

E. Well, it's *silly*. It's—it's just a feeling—it—it—maybe it's because I know she doesn't want me to go . . . and she's just been after me all week not to go . . . and it's a—she's just been after me and after me and . . . I just can't find any reason not to go.

DR. F. Now just move ahead in time and see yourself getting dressed at the count of five. One . . . two . . . three . . . four . . . five and what comes to mind?

E. All the kids are in my room and they're playing on the bed . . . and watching me get dressed and they're all happy . . . they would like to go . . . ah . . . [Her voice softening.] I would take them. I should take them. She's being unreasonable. I'm— I'm just getting dressed.

DR. F. Tell me what you're doing.

E. Well, I'm—I'm putting on my corset and John, the oldest, is tying it up and he really gets a kick out of that. [She smiles.] Ah . . . let's see . . . now I'm going to fix my hair and . . . just get dressed.

DR. F. What do you decide about the children? At the count of three. One . . . two . . . three.

E. Well, I think—I think I would like to take them— I—I—I'm going to go down and talk to her about that. [Becoming determined.] They'll have a good time and there's other children there and we live so far out of town . . . and they don't get to see them very often . . . and I would like to take them.

DR. F. All right. Now see yourself talking to your sister-in-law at the count of three. One . . . two . . . three and what comes to mind?

E. She's in the kitchen . . . doing busy work because she's angry. [Inhaling deeply.] Ah . . . no, she doesn't want the kids to go . . . and she doesn't want me to go and . . . she doesn't want anybody to go to—I don't know why she's so angry. She's just so negative . . . and she can't give me a reason why. She just doesn't want them to go . . . and then she's just doing it out of spite. They just had their bath and they're all ready for bed and this and that . . . [With annoyance.] And ah . . . it's not fair!

DR. F. I'd like you to move ahead to the moment when you're leaving at the count of three. One . . . two . . . three. What are you aware of?

E. I'm out on the . . . out on the front porch . . . ah . . . oh, that's it. David's going to come and pick

70

me up . . . and ah . . . he lives over on the next farm . . . and I'm still trying to talk her into going . . . [Deep sigh.] . . . and I can't get rid of that feeling that I shouldn't go . . . and it's just a normal goodbye.

DR. F. How is David taking you? What is he taking you in?

E. In the wagon . . . his wagon.

DR. F. Is anybody else there with him?

E. No, just us. He's—he lives over on the next farm and ah . . . there's just him and his father and they work the farm . . . and his father's quite old . . . we've been neighbors forever.

DR. F. Now move ahead to some event at the party at the count of three. One . . . two . . . three and what comes to mind?

E. We're in the parlor and everybody's there. And everybody's having such a good time and . . . it's just—just a good time. Just a good time. There's dancing and there's singing.

DR. F. Are you having a good time too?

E. Oh yeah . . . yeah. Yeah. I'm the schoolteacher and I know everybody . . . and all the kids . . . all the kids are having such a good time . . . and I think I'll give an assignment on the party.

DR. F. All right. Now I'd like you to move ahead to the next significant event at the count of three. One . . . two . . . three and what comes to mind?

E. I'm still at the party . . . I—we were there quite late and we're getting ready to leave now. It must be midnight or one o'clock and . . . we're just coming home. [Deep sigh.] I'm a little worried about coming home.

DR. F. Why is that?

E. That feeling never went away. I shouldn't have gone. She was *so* unhappy.

DR. F. All right, now, let's see if anything happens during the ride . . . anything that is important for you to know about at the count of three. One . . . two . . . three and what comes to mind?

E. Hmm . . . David asked me to marry him. Wonder why he wasn't important? [Mumbling.]

DR. F. What did you say?

E. He's not important. I don't love him. I—he's a friend and . . . I don't want to marry him. I don't want to marry anybody. And so we have a discussion about that. I don't think he loves me either. He just wants a companion. His father is old and . . . he just wants a companion.

DR. F. What do you say to him?

E. I just tell him that. I don't—I don't think we should get married just to have someone to marry . . . and he understands. He—he—he's just lonesome . . . and I told him, "We'll just be friends," . . . and that's all. It was surprising though. He must be very lonely.

DR. F. Now move ahead to the next significant event at the count of five. One . . . two . . . three . . . four . . . five.

E. Okay . . . all right. [Breathing rapidly.] David's gone home . . . I hear this person running in the woods . . . it's black . . . no moon . . . and I go up the walk to the house . . . and the front door is open . . . it's dark inside . . . there's a doll on the floor. The doll has curly hair . . . there's a . . . I'm standing in the, like a living room. Um . . . I don't know what comes next. [Sounding frightened.] There's the stairs. There's no candle. There's no light. There's supposed to be a candle by the—on the table by the front door and there's no candle . . . and it's dark, dark . . . and I go upstairs . . . [Deep sigh.] . . . and I go upstairs . . . [Trembling violently.]

DR. F. Where are you going when you go upstairs?

E. It's that attic door!

DR. F. Go on.

E. [Long pause.] Only it's not an attic, it's my bedroom. [Deep sigh—shudders.] Okay. [Bravely.] I go—I go upstairs . . . I'm walking up the stairs . . . and they're wet . . . they're wet. [Whispered.] It's—it's blood. [Shuddering again.]

72

DR. F. What are you thinking about this blood?

E. [Covering her eyes.] I don't think anything . . . I . . .

DR. F. What are you feeling?

E. Sick!

DR. F. All right . . . keep going.

E. Okay. I . . . I go up the stairs and . . . the door is shut . . . the door's shut. [Whispered.] I *can't* open that door. [Crying.] I can't open that door. [Shuddered sigh.] I've got to open that door . . . maybe in a minute. [Long pause.] I'm standing in front of the door . . . I am *so* scared . . . there isn't a sound anywhere! I know I opened the door. Why can't I open that door now? [Gripping the arms of the chair.]

DR. F. You'll be able to. You just gave yourself one minute and that minute isn't up yet. Just take a deep breath, really deep breath, deep, deep breath.

E. [Sound of deep breaths.] Okay . . . okay . . . [Covering her eyes again.] I can't!

DR. F. Yes, you can. You did it before. You can do it again.

E. I know what's behind that door!

DR. F. Open it up. What do you think is behind that door? What is behind the door?

E. [Wailing.] Everyone . . . in . . . that . . . house . . . is sliced up . . . and I can't look at it again. [Twists her whole body away.]

DR. F. Yes, you can. You have to do it.

E. [Sounds of pathetic sobbing.]

DR. F. [I take her hand in mine, stroking it.] You're not alone. I'm here with you. Open the door and tell me what you see. Stay calm and relaxed. Calm and relaxed. It's all right. Tell me what you see. You can do it . . . this is your big chance.

E. [Becoming brave and facing forward again.] All right . . . I just won't look down.

DR. F. Just do it whatever way is easiest. And what do you do?

E. I opened it . . . I just rushed and I opened that door. [Deep, shuddering sob.] And the door hit something . . . and I open the door and . . . and the mother's—the door hit the mother's head . . . and it—it—it rolled . . . [Hardly able to talk.] . . . and there was . . . the mother . . . and . . . and [Sobbing.] . . . and the three children . . . and they were cut up . . . and their arms and legs were off . . . and their heads were off . . . and there was blood everywhere . . . and it just kept looking at me . . . they kept looking at me and . . . I fainted . . . and I got sick and I couldn't go anywhere and I couldn't find my way out . . . and that—that head kept looking at me and looking at me . . . and the place smelled like blood everywhere . . . and he just *butchered* them! And he cut them open. He just cut everywhere! And he tore out their insides that he cut—he mutilated them. [Gasping.] There—there was nothing that was not destroyed in that room . . . everything was destroyed in that room. Who was it that did that? Who could do a thing like that? [Looking horrified—hysterical—covering her face.] No!

DR. F. Who came to mind?

E. Her husband . . . my brother . . . he couldn't do that . . . he couldn't do that . . . [Sobbing inconsolably.] . . . he couldn't do that . . . I just can't accept that . . . but . . . no! [Shaking her head.]

DR. F. Relax now.

E. [Long pause.] It had to be him. [Resigned.] There was nobody else . . . and I was coming home and . . . and I heard him run out the door . . . and I ran in the house . . . the doll was laying there and there was *blood* all down the stairs. [Now breaking down into uncontrollable sobs.] I wish I didn't . . . why did I have to go? [Pleadingly.] Can I leave now?

DR. F. Where are you?

E. I don't want to be here.

DR. F. Where are you now?

E. I'm downstairs.

DR. F. Are you alone or are you with someone?

E. I'm alone. [Sounding exhausted.] I have to get into

town somehow. We live about five miles out of town.

DR. F. You want to leave? You don't want to be in that place with . . .

E. I don't want to be there. [Almost child-like.]

DR. F. All right, let's see what happens.

E. Nothing happens.

DR. F. What are you doing right now?

E. I'm throwing up . . . all over the place . . . I'm just trying to get outside . . . and I just wish I hadn't come home and . . . I just am *so* confused . . . and ah . . . [Sinking deeper into the chair.]

DR. F. Did you see anyone leaving? You said you heard someone running through the woods.

E. I heard him run out the back door and through the woods as I was coming up and ah . . . there was nobody else there. It—I just *know* that he never came back . . . and I just know that's who it was . . . [Nodding, wiping her eyes.] It was my brother.

DR. F. What do you mean, "He never came back"?

E. He never came back. They never found him. He never came back. [Big sigh.] And ah . . . that's all. I just don't know any more.

DR. F. Why would he do a thing like that?

E. [Long pause.]

DR. F. What comes to mind?

E. The only thing that comes to mind is *being drunk.*

DR. F. Does he get drunk often?

E. Yes . . . now I go out on the porch.

DR. F. Then what?

E. I go into town.

DR. F. How do you get there?

E. Walk.

DR. F. At night?

E. Um-hmm.

DR. F. Is there a moon?

E. No . . . it's dark.

DR. F. Are you frightened?

E. I'm sick! I'm not frightened. There's nothing in the world anybody could do to me . . . that could hurt me any more than that . . . I don't want to have to go and tell them.

DR. F. Is it a long walk?

E. It's all right . . . I have nothing else to do.

DR. F. What are you doing now?

E. I'm just walking . . . and . . . I'm just walking. [Crying again.]

DR. F. Now I'm going to count from one to five and on the count of five, you'll be in town. One . . . two . . . three . . . four . . . five and what do you do now?

E. I go to the sheriff's house.

DR. F. Yes?

E. And I go and . . . [Shaking her head.] I can't tell him what's happened.

DR. F. Tell *me* what is happening.

E. I'm in already. I just and . . . now I'm in . . . and I can't tell him what's happened.

DR. F. What does he say to you?

E. Well, he wants to know how I got so bloody . . . and . . . I tell him, "I can't tell you, but you've *got* to go out to the farm . . . and I can't go with you . . . I can't go back there . . ." And then his wife comes and takes me upstairs and cleans me up and puts me to bed . . . and they send for the doctor. [Sighing.] And ah . . . and I have a drink of whiskey and she sits by me . . . and . . . the doctor looks at me and says I'm all right . . . and then I just go to bed and die . . . I just don't want to live anymore. [Taking a big breath.] But, I have to. I have to . . . and . . . then there's an investigation . . . and questions.

DR. F. Who investigates?

E. The sheriff.

DR. F. Does he investigate *you*, Sarah? Does he ask you a lot of questions?

E. Yeah. He asks—well, he knows I was in town . . . and—at this party. Anyway, and they ask questions and I answer questions and I tell them everything I know and then that's over . . . and I leave.

DR. F. Do they ask about your brother?

E. Yeah.

DR. F. What do they say? What questions do they ask you?

E. Where he was.

DR. F. What did you say?

E. I said that as far as I knew he was on this other farm. [Big sigh.] But apparently he wasn't there. And that's why I think he did it. And I didn't know who it was that ran . . . I honestly didn't know who it was . . . I couldn't say who it was.

DR. F. Yet when you saw those bodies, the thought occurred to you that it was your brother, didn't it?

E. He's *so* easily angered.

DR. F. Has he ever been violent before?

E. He's very hard on his animals. He can wear a horse out in five years. He's just a hard, hard man who doesn't have a lot of sympathy.

DR. F. Did he have a knife?

E. Oh, yeah. Everybody has to have a knife.

DR. F. What happened after the investigation? Did you ever go back to that farm?

E. No!

DR. F. What did they do with the bodies?

E. [Completely dejected.] I don't know . . . I guess they buried them.

DR. F. What did you do after that?

E. I didn't go to the funeral . . . I couldn't.

DR. F. What did you do?

E. I just left . . . I stayed in town for a while . . . until everybody was . . . I couldn't go to that funeral. I just couldn't. [Breathing deeply.] And . . . I guess I just went . . . a little bit crazy . . .

DR. F. Tell me more, if you can.

E. It seems to me . . . they put me in an insane asylum . . . it was horrible . . . [Shuddering.] I don't want to think about that . . . I was there the rest of my life.

DR. F. Now I'm going to ask you to remember this when you wake up. It's very important for this to be part of your conscious mind. Know that you have opened the attic door. Haven't you? You've uncovered all the horrors deep within you that have kept you feeling so

77

anxious when you're away from your children . . . and when you come back at night. Do you understand now why it was hard for you to have a good time either at a party or away from them? Afraid when you came back that they'd be stabbed . . . remember when we talked about that?

E. Um-hmm.

DR. F. Afraid to enjoy sex?

E. [Nods her head yes.]

DR. F. In other words you didn't feel that you deserved to have a good time . . . because before, when you had a good time, look what happened.

E. I should never have gone.

DR. F. It would have happened if you had stayed home. Be realistic.

E. Well . . . he might have killed me too . . . but I might have also hit him a good one, too.

DR. F. Was your sister-in-law a weak woman?

E. Yes. I was ah . . . quite a bit bigger than she is . . . was. I wasn't huge, but I was a strong girl, who worked all her life on the farm. She was raised in town . . . and also I knew how to handle my brother.

DR. F. So you feel that if you were there you might have prevented that from happening?

E. Yeah. Somebody might have gotten hurt . . . but nobody would have gotten killed.

DR. F. All right. I just want to tell you this. You weren't there and it isn't your responsibility. You have to feel free now. Free of the guilt. You have no reason to feel guilty any longer. You didn't commit those crimes.

E. I *feel* like I did.

DR. F. Well, you didn't do it. You didn't commit those crimes and if you had been there and your brother was absolutely out of his head, as he must have been to do that horrible thing, you would have been killed too. You would have been one more dead. There's no way you could have stopped him. You know the violence that it took to sever those heads and to do all those destructive things. He would not have stopped.

78

He had a knife, you weren't armed. There is no way . . .

E. Maybe she . . . said something to set him off . . . I don't know. [She starts to cry again.]

DR. F. Nobody will ever know. The point is that you could not have stopped him. All that would have happened is that you would have gotten killed, too. Now you know deep within yourself that it takes a tremendous amount of strength and violence to sever a head and to do the kinds of things he did. And those were his *own* children. So that his love for his children didn't stop him and certainly his sister's command or efforts wouldn't have stopped him either.

E. I know that . . . but I still feel *so* responsible.

DR. F. Well, would you be willing to give up that feeling of responsibility now? And also to know that probably the moment that he started after those people, their consciousness left the body, that their essence was not harmed?

E. Do you really think so?

DR. F. I really think so. I believe that. It has been shown that sometimes when people are in extreme danger, the consciousness leaves the body, so they're not touched, they don't even feel it.

E. I hope that's true.

DR. F. Now Elizabeth, I want to ask you, is your brother anyone you know in this lifetime?

E. [Silence.]

DR. F. Who is your brother? What comes to mind at the count of three? One . . . two . . . three and what comes to mind?

E. My father.

DR. F. And who is your sister-in-law? At the count of three. One . . . two . . . three.

E. My mother.

DR. F. And the children. Do you know them in this lifetime?

E. [Whispered.] They are mine.

DR. F. Does this fit with anything you know about your father?

79

E. He has a violent nature.

DR. F. Is your mother afraid of your father?

E. Yes!

DR. F. What about your children? Are they afraid of him?

E. I ah . . . watch that very carefully. When he's upset, I take my children away.

DR. F. All right. Now you know why. All the things are fitting into place, aren't they? Now, when you remember this when you are home, you're going to feel calm and relaxed. You will be very calm and relaxed. Between now and next week, you will receive more and more insights from this regression. Now I'm going to count from ten to zero and I want you to come back to Elizabeth, completely back to yourself. Bring forward these memories, it's important for you to do that. You have been very courageous today. I want to tell you how wonderful I think you were to face that. It would have been easy to run away. Ten . . . nine . . . eight . . . seven . . . six . . . five . . . four . . . three . . . two . . . one . . . zero.

Back to the present, by now deeply hypnotized, Elizabeth put her hand to her head and moaned, "My head aches." (No wonder!) I gave her hypnotic suggestions that eliminated the pain. Then I brought her out of the trance.

Surprisingly, she smiled at me. I smiled back. We had really been through something together. I felt very close to her. She told me of always being afraid of her father, who, it turned out, drank heavily. She alluded to an incident in which he beat her, ". . . but I don't have the strength to go into it. I just want to flop in bed for the rest of the afternoon." She got up and said, "Well, if this is it, it will be put to the test tomorrow." "What do you mean?" I asked. She explained, "My husband and I are going to a play in San Francisco. I've been worried about it all week." Just before she left, I asked her to share her regression with her husband—but not her children. I wanted to be sure none of it became repressed again, even though she seemed able to handle it well, once she got it out. Then I suggested she make a list of all the ways her life as Sarah had affected her—in this lifetime.

At our next session, Elizabeth was smiling broadly at me, in a cheery Indian print sun dress. She commented as she walked from the waiting room, "I feel great!"

I complimented her on her dress. "I made it myself—and am making another. I even feel comfortable being this bare," she said with a delighted look on her face. She pointed out the ruffles on the bottom of the dress. I observed that she must have put a lot of effort into making it.

After settling herself in the chair, she looked at me for a few seconds with a straight face. Then she broke out into a big open smile and said with obvious relish, "It worked! Chris and I went to that show in San Francisco. I had a good time. And I didn't worry at all about the children. I walked right in when we got home, before I realized what I had done."

Before I could finish telling her how happy I was about that, she interrupted, eager to continue with the good news. "I needed to pick up my daughter the other night. She was at a nearby library. It meant leaving my two younger kids alone." She paused. "So I did!" She left her children unattended for about a half-hour, something she had never done. She admitted that they told her they were a little scared. I commented that they were probably reacting because they had been overprotected for so many years. Also I felt they may be resonating at a subconscious level to a time, probably over a hundred years ago when they were left by her. And that time it proved fatal! We discussed sharing what Elizabeth had learned about that life with them—and decided against it for now for a number of reasons. Her daughter's therapist was away on a trip. And her other children would probably need help, too, when their repression weakened—which would be the reason for telling them. They might prove to be even more resistant than their mother, because of the violence they had endured. Undoubtedly it would be even harder for them. I would have to set aside more time for them than my schedule permitted right now. I thought about my calender, knowing I would have no room for new patients for at least six months. No, we would have to wait.

Elizabeth had brought two pages of yellow legal paper filled with notes—notes that drew careful parallels between Sarah's life and hers, adding conclusions and insights. She included comments on her children and how they had been affected. She began reading:

> My first serious depression began when we made plans to move out of California. I looked forward to living in the East. I'm still captivated by it. The depression became very deep when we finally moved to Pennsylvania. I was far away and felt I couldn't get home if I were needed. I couldn't help Mom if she needed me. As a child, I was my mother's protector. I still am! Many times (when I was older) I would battle my father to help my mother. I'm intimidated by him. I fear and love him at the same time. We have a rapport that is very close. Daddy used to tell me I was the only one who understood him. This was especially true after we had violent encounters.

She stopped, putting the pages down on her lap. "My father's always been an alcoholic." Tears sprang to her eyes as she continued. "We've had some violent fights. The worst time I can remember was when I was just a kid. I must have been eleven—no, maybe thirteen—sometime in those years. Well, my father had been out all night. It was morning. I was still in bed. He started in on my mother. He belittled her. Then he threatened her life. I came out and told him if he hated us so much to get out! Never come back! I screamed at him. It shocked him. He looked at the door. Then he left. I told Mom never to let him back again. He came back a few days later. He *terrorized* us! He demolished the house! He broke everything! He left—went to another state." Her fists were clenched, as she added through her teeth, "She took him back!"

I suggested she close her eyes and relax for a few minutes. I gave her some calming suggestions and then brought her up to an awake state.

She picked up her notes. "I'll tell you about the children," she said. Then reading, "Mark, thirteen, has an uncomfortable feeling about being upstairs alone at night. Even if someone is asleep upstairs, he still feels he is alone. The girls cannot stand to have anything pointed at their heads, especially at their foreheads between their eyes." I told her that this is a common finding. When a person is severely injured or killed by blows or shots in the head in a past life, he or she will report the same kind of sensitivity. I asked her to read on. "My girls can 'read' my Dad's moods. They have learned how to say things to him. Mark is more blunt— but he's still very aware of my father's sensibilities. They don't like to be alone. And I never leave them with him—even for a minute. I just realized that this week."

After she got her things together to leave, she smiled, gave me a big hug and said, "I'm still flabbergasted at how simple it's been!"

The following week Elizabeth came in a brightly colored dress, reflecting her friendly, cheerful mood. The week had gone remarkably well. She and her family had attended an air show, which she enjoyed. Her parents came for the weekend to accompany them. "Something's changed in me. I watched my mother and my father all weekend. I'm not their daughter anymore. Not in the sense I was," she said, frowning. "The biggest shocker was my mother. She always had been my confidante. I told her about the regression. She denied that it was real. She tried to get me to stop talking about it. She told me, 'Leave it all alone!' Now I realize how depressed she is herself. I can't expect her to be understanding. Now there's no *real* closeness. Part of my life is shut off. I watched my Dad. His biggest joy is criticizing other people. When I was a kid we never did anything interesting—no parades, no outings. Nothing! He spent this past weekend criticizing people because they were doing something." She brightened up as she announced, "It's a new realization to me. Up till now I was patterning our life after how it had been for me. It was very traumatic for me realizing all this. I don't have to fit any standards anymore. But back to the air show—I had a damn good time! But it's sad. I realize all these years that I've been holding back."

I asked her, "How do you feel when you think or talk about the regression?" She smiled again and replied, "I'm not so bothered by the grisly details." She looked off for a few moments, deep in thought. Then she said, "Things are getting solved that were never solved before. I just feel it. I feel more comfortable with myself as a person. The changes are internal ones. But Chris does notice I'm more relaxed. I can't describe it, but it's a feeling inside myself."

She checked the clock on the small teak table next to her chair. We had twenty minutes left. "Would you make me a weight tape?" I agreed and put her in a trance. I asked her to visualize herself on the scales at one hundred and thirty, her ideal weight. Then I had her visualize herself in front of a full-length mirror at this ideal weight, enjoying looking one by one at the various parts of her slim body. I brought her out of hypnosis, handed her the tape and said, "Have a good week."

For the third week in a row, Elizabeth came for our appointment in a dress, this time a very attractive, blue and white sun dress. She was also wearing new white sandals and stockings. Even her hair looked cut and styled.

"There's a big change in me. I made reservations to go away for two nights. And I feel no anxiety about the trip. I asked the kids to make arrangements to stay with their friends for the weekend. But what surprised me the most is my attitude with them. My oldest daughter was going through her martyr bit and I was able to be assertive with her. I didn't even get angry or upset." Smiling, obviously very pleased, she said, "It's really fantastic! I can't get over the fact that it was so damn easy with them. There was no guilt. It was so simple! *I* feel in control. Before, those kids could really manipulate me. I was always tired of forever trying to soothe someone's hurt feelings." She talked of feeling comfortable making mistakes—not embarrassed. She punctuated it with, "It's all right now to make a mistake! There's no reason why I can't make a mistake."

Changing the topic, she discussed her sex life, which had also greatly improved. Then she remarked, "You know, we really enjoyed it before the kids. I'm not inhibited about sex. It's just I couldn't let myself go. I was always listening for the children." With a grin, she said, "This trip will be a two-day honeymoon!"

"Oh, guess what! I've lost six pounds in one week!" she announced.

As she stood by my desk, ready to leave, she reflected, "You know, the first week after the regression, I was completely amazed. My emotions were totally different. I was in control for the first time I can remember. My personality is the same, but my attitude is different."

It has been almost six months since Elizabeth's first session. Working with her has been challenging, exciting, suspenseful and extremely rewarding for me. I have thoroughly enjoyed watching—and helping—her drama unfold. I have also grown very fond of her. I was delighted one day to hear that she had cancelled her appointments for one month. She planned to treat herself to one week alone in Hawaii and spend the remaining three weeks with Chris, taking "mini-vacations." We shall continue to work together until she feels free of irrational fears and anxieties, and totally comfortable with herself. This, I view as the "mop-up" operation. The worst is over.

CHAPTER FIVE

✖

"On the Ship Everybody Is Hungry"

William's face was tense and flushed as he settled himself carefully into the reclining chair opposite me. His problem was obvious—obesity—100 surplus pounds of it. He could not conceal many of his 245 pounds because his five-foot, five-inch frame left no room for hiding them. Despite his weight, he was an attractive man in his late twenties. He sported a stylish beard and sideburns and had a well-groomed look about him.

He spoke with a tone of futility and his voice became wheezy as he told me, "I was fat as a baby and I was a fat kid until the fifth grade. Then I started growing and reached my full height—that helped some." He said that he had a few years of being only slightly overweight. Then the pounds piled on. He weighed close to 200 pounds when he started college at eighteen. He had always felt conspicuous, being the only overweight person in his very weight-conscious family. "Diets have come to be a way of life for me—but sticking to them has been absolutely impossible." He added, "I find myself eating food I detest and, in an evening, I catch myself staring at the refrigerator—at least ten times. It's such a struggle not to give in."

Several weeks before our first appointment, William had begun still another calorie diet and was doing well on it. He pointed out, "Breaking 200 pounds is the real challenge, because for years I've been unable to get below 205 despite everything—shots, pills, Weight Watchers and all the diets." Like most of my obese patients, he is an expert on the full range of diets.

As William continued to tell me why he had come for help, I learned that he had a host of allergies and had

86

been asthmatic since birth. He had had the usual tests, and was on medication to control his reactions. He was sensitive to chicken feathers and cat fur, as well as other domestic animals' fur. He recounted a long list of allergens, but noted, "I've never been the slightest bit allergic to wild animals' fur. Isn't that strange?" I wondered to myself if his allergies could be traced to something that had once happened to him. If so, he might get much more than he had bargained for out of his hypnotherapy. I decided to wait and see, rather than to share my hunch with him. I could not risk planting a suggestion and I did not want to disappoint him in case my hunch did not pan out.

We ended the session after I taught him self-hypnosis, making him a tape to practice with at home. We set up an appointment for the next week. He left saying, "I've promised myself, I'm going to stick it out this time until I'm down to 145."

The following week William reported that he had played the self-hypnosis tape diligently several times each day. "I really feel so much more relaxed. I'm sure my blood pressure is down some, too. I seem to go deeper each time I listen to it. Is that normal?" I nodded and replied, "That's exactly what we want. Soon, without the tape, you will be able to just close your eyes, tell yourself, 'Relax now, William' and you'll be deeply hypnotized. Then you can give yourself any kind of suggestions that are important to you at the time—for your weight, to relax before giving a talk, in case of pain. But, let's talk more about that later. We have work to do today."

William slipped into a deep trance immediately as I began the induction. I questioned him about his obesity. His inner mind indicated by his finger signals that his weight problem had subconscious roots. One was tied to a traumatic birth this time around. I gave him suggestions to "go back to just a few minutes before you are born. At the count of five you will relive that experience. One . . . Two . . . Three . . . four . . . five." He grimaced. His body squirmed in the chair. "My head! . . . It's being squeezed. I feel like I'm

being crushed . . . oh . . . my chest! Ohhh . . . I
hear screaming . . . it's my mother . . . oh, no . . .
my mother's screaming." After he was "born," he relaxed. I helped him to know that her pain was not his
fault and suggested that he free himself from the guilt
he had carried. Then I brought him back to the present,
staying deeply relaxed. I asked him about the other
event. His inner mind slowly revealed that it had occurred in a previous lifetime. But he was not ready to
deal with any more that week. I gave him suggestions
that he prepare himself, at a subconscious level, during
the interval between appointments. His "yes" finger
hesitantly lifted, indicating his subconscious mind's co-
operation.

The following week, I regressed William to a "particularly significant event in the past" that was related to
his weight problem. His body began to tremble. His
voice was so weak that I had to strain to hear him:

w. It's been very calm . . . no wind . . . there's not
   enough food. On the ship everybody is hungry . . .
   maybe even sick.

DR. F. Everybody's hungry and everybody's sick?

w. Yes . . . it's scurvy.

DR. F. How do you feel?

w. [His voice is wavering.] Hungry.

DR. F. How long has it been since you've eaten?

w. We have some food, but it's just a little porridge or
   something.

DR. F. But it's not enough?

w. No.

DR. F. Have you lost a lot of weight?

w. Yes . . . I don't know how much in weight, but my
   arms and my ribs are sticking out . . . we're starving.

DR. F. Are you worried about yourself?

w. Yes . . . I don't think I ever knew how much I
   weighed.

DR. F. But you were healthy before this happened?

w. Yeah.

DR. F. Just tell me what else you see and what you're aware of.

W. Like the inside of the crew's quarters, the fo'c'sle . . . and there are people on hammocks and . . . and everybody is just there.

DR. F. How do you feel?

W. I'm sick . . . and their eyes are all sunken in.

DR. F. Has anyone died of starvation?

W. . . . I think so.

DR. F. Where are you?

W. We're in the ship.

DR. F. What's the name of your ship?

W. Sally.

DR. F. Sally? Is there another name?

W. Yeah.

DR. F. What is it?

W. May—the *Sally May*.

DR. F. Where are you?

W. It's the Atlantic.

DR. F. Where are you going?

W. I don't know.

DR. F. Where did you come from? Where is your home?

W. From America.

DR. F. What place in America?

W. New England.

DR. F. What part did you come from?

W. Bedford, Massachusetts.

DR. F. Who are you?

W. Tom.

DR. F. What's your last name?

W. Jones.

DR. F. How old are you?

W. Not very old.

DR. F. Are you under twenty?

W. No, just over.

DR. F. You're just over twenty?

W. A couple of years, maybe.

DR. F. Are you married?

W. I think so.

DR. F. What is your wife's name?

W. Jean.

DR. F. What is the year?

W. Seventeen . . . seventeen eighty-one.

DR. F. Move forward in time to an important event. One . . . two . . . three.

W. [Lowering his voice.] I think I took something I wasn't supposed to.

DR. F. What did you do with it?

W. I ate it. [Becoming upset.]

DR. F. What was it?

W. A chicken.

DR. F. Where was that chicken?

W. It was in the storage . . . [Whispering.] It was for the officers.

DR. F. Was it a live chicken that was kept there?

W. Yes, there were lots of them.

DR. F. They were for the officers?

W. Yes. [With an angry look on his face.]

DR. F. Tell me what you did with the chicken. How did you take it?

W. [Breathing very rapidly.]

DR. F. Stay calm and relaxed. There's no need to get upset. How do you feel within yourself right now?

W. A little scared.

DR. F. What are you afraid of?

W. I don't know . . . maybe I'll get caught. [Trembling.]

DR. F. How did you catch this chicken?

W. I snuck in and took it while there was nobody there . . . and I took it away to the front of the ship . . . and I'm sure I must have killed it somehow, but I don't know.

DR. F. See yourself killing it.

W. [Long pause.] I wring its neck.

DR. F. And then what do you do with it?

W. I skin it and . . . I tear it open with my fingers and . . . it's awful . . . the smell of the guts. [Grimacing.] I feel like vomiting . . . finally, I cooked it.

DR. F. How could you cook it?

W. I . . . don't . . . know.

DR. F. The knowledge will come.

90

w. There was a lantern . . . I cooked it with that.

DR. F. How did that chicken taste to you?

w. Good. [Smiling.]

DR. F. And now let's proceed to the next important event. One . . . two . . . three. [Pause.] What happened?

w. [Evasively.] I was punished.

DR. F. They caught you?

w. Yes.

DR. F. Who caught you?

w. One of the officers.

DR. F. What did he say to you?

w. He cursed at me . . . and he hit me, and he grabbed me and dragged me. [Breathing hard.]

DR. F. Where did he drag you?

w. Towards the captain's cabin. [Shaking violently.]

DR. F. How do you feel?

w. [His breathing very labored, whispering.] Afraid!

DR. F. And then what happened?

w. They say they're gonna beat me . . . I'm gonna get lashes. [His voice filled with stark terror.]

DR. F. Become calm and relaxed at the count of three. One . . . two . . . three. When do they do it?

w. A little later—I think it's the next day.

DR. F. Who was watching?

w. Everybody, the whole ship's company.

DR. F. What else comes to you?

w. Just the vision of being hit.

DR. F. What did they beat you with?

w. [Flinching.] With a cat-o'-nine.

DR. F. How many times did they hit you?

w. Thirty. [Squirming in the chair, his face bathed in sweat.]

It took many minutes of calming suggestions before William was sufficiently relaxed to continue. I brought him back to the present so that he could look at what had happened. He shuddered when he looked back on the relived trauma of sneaking up to the officers' area to get his meal. With amazement in his voice, he put

91

together the pieces of the puzzle—the buried memory of starving that had been haunting him all these years.

I brought him out of the trance. He shook his head in bewilderment. "Did I really experience another lifetime? I'm not even sure I believe we live more than once." He explained, "Even though I have doubts about all that, I do pride myself on having an open mind. This will have to sink in."

When he came in for his next appointment the following week, he announced, "I have discovered something remarkable this week! My wife and I were having dinner at a restaurant. And for the first time ever, I ordered something because I liked it—not because it would be the largest quantity of food! All these years I have been eating like a starving man!" He also described his fascination with ships, especially shipwrecks and history. (While under hypnosis, on another occasion, he revealed he was a sailor in *three* different lifetimes.) During the week, he had had a flash of insight. The incident he had recalled during his regression as Tom had occurred while the *Sally May* was becalmed at sea while stalking British ships, a few years after the Revolutionary War. His check with some history books showed that type of warfare was not unusual, even after 1776.

Under hypnosis, his subconscious mind brought to light that he had been at sea most of his years during that lifetime and lived to be an old man. Although he never starved again, an indelible impression had been left—one that persisted for almost two hundred years.

During another of our hypnoanalytic sessions, William's subconscious mind disclosed that some of his allergies were due to emotional experiences in his present life (as well as physical intolerances to certain foods), while others originated in a past life.

While he was still deep in a trance, I regressed him to the events in the former lifetime responsible for his allergy to cat fur. Again we meet Tom Jones:

w. Two things . . . I was eating a chicken . . . and the cat found me. It wanted some, and I wouldn't

92

give it any. I kicked it and it started to yell and scream . . . and people came and found me with the chicken. [Beginning to wheeze slightly.]

DR. F. So it was the cat that caused you to be discovered with the chicken?

W. Yes . . . I didn't want to get found. [Breathing rapidly.]

DR. F. And being found caused you a great deal of anxiety, didn't it?

W. That was the other cat.

DR. F. What other cat?

W. The cat-o'-nine-tails.

DR. F. Tell me about it.

W. It's a whip and they beat me with it.

DR. F. How many strokes?

W. [His body jerks violently and repeatedly.] Thirty times and it had little balls on the end . . . and they tear into your flesh . . . [Gasping for air.] . . . and then when it's all over, they put sea water on the open wounds. [Exhausted.]

DR. F. How do you feel right now?

W. [Trembling.] Afraid.

DR. F. And what are you afraid of?

W. Pain.

DR. F. The pain is all over, you don't have to be afraid of it anymore. Stay calm and relaxed. At the count of five you will be very calm and very relaxed. One . . . two . . . three . . . four . . . five.

A check with his finger signals verified that his allergy to chicken feathers was conditioned by the fear he felt as he caught the chicken and his disgust as he ripped off its feathers and disemboweled it.

Each day, beginning with our first session, William meticulously plotted his weight on a graph. Our custom had been to inspect this chart first thing each time we met. The weight line was making a struggling, downward trip. William was continuing to lose weight at the rate of about three pounds a week. His chart reflected his loss and finally reached 200 pounds. But then a curious thing happened—he developed an incredible craving for chocolate! It became so persistent that he found himself drawn each day like a magnet to fast-food shops, where he felt compelled to buy several chocolate bars. "I can resist everything else, but this is wrecking my 800-calorie-a-day diet." He experienced the usual guilt, self-hate and promises to himself that almost invariably follow such transgressions. "But I can't stop. Chocolates are completely irresistible—and, of course, one is never enough." We decided to do something about it.

Under hypnosis, I asked his subconscious mind if there were something at an inner mind level responsible for this craving. His "yes" finger slowly lifted. "Is there an event from this life that is involved?" This time his "no" finger responded. I regressed him "to an event a long time ago that has to do with your craving for chocolate."

w. Well . . . there's darkness all around me. I can't seem to see anything.

DR. F. In a few moments it will become very clear to you what is happening.

w. [Sadly.] It's cold . . . it's dark and cold.

DR. F. What are you doing?

w. Kind of huddled up because it's so cold. [Shivering.]

DR. F. Where are you?

w. I'm outside. It's snowing, and I think . . . I think there's rocks and trees, mostly rocks and kind of like a rock grotto or something . . . and it's snowing and cold.

DR. F. Just get in touch with who you are. You'll know your name and all about yourself.

w. I was hunting . . . and I'm lost and I think I'm gonna freeze! I don't know my name. [Voice very raspy and shaky.]

DR. F. On the count of three you will. One . . . two . . . three.

w. Fred.

DR. F. Fred, you got lost . . . you were hunting and you got lost?

94

w. Yes.

DR. F. How long have you been lost?

w. All day . . . I started in the morning and I was planning to be done by noon and I got lost, and it's night. [Completely baffled.]

DR. F. Where are you? What country or what state?

w. I'm . . . I think I'm in the United States . . . I'm hunting for deer.

DR. F. Do you live near where you went hunting?

w. I don't think I live around here too close . . . maybe twenty miles.

DR. F. Were you hunting with friends or by yourself?

w. I was . . . I was just walking by myself . . . and I . . . and I don't know, all of a sudden things looked strange, and I got lost. I don't know how . . .

DR. F. What is the name of where you live?

w. Idaho.

DR. F. Have you been hunting for deer many times before?

w. Yes, and I never got lost. [Said with obvious pride.]

DR. F. Fred, how old are you?

w. I'm about thirty.

DR. F. And what's the year?

w. Nineteen-oh-five.

DR. F. What kind of gun is that that you have?

w. It's a Stevens.

DR. F. Is it a rifle?

w. Yes.

DR. F. Did you bring any food with you?

w. No, I thought I'd be back for lunch.

DR. F. Who is back at your home?

w. Nobody . . . just me.

DR. F. You live by yourself?

w. Yes. I have a cabin.

DR. F. Do you live in that cabin or is that just for hunting?

w. I live there. I can't figure out why I'm lost. It's . . . it's dumb!

DR. F. Now I'd like you to just go ahead in time a few minutes or to the next important thing that happens.

w. Somebody's coming . . . it's a person on a horse. [His voice vibrating with excitement.]

DR. F. What do you do?

w. I yell at him.

DR. F. What do you say?

w. I say, "Hey, stop!" and I ask him where I am.

DR. F. What does he say?

w. I don't know . . . I can't understand.

DR. F. You can't understand? Why is that?

w. I don't know.

DR. F. Is this the same night?

w. It's the next day.

DR. F. What does this man look like?

w. He's about . . . five and a half feet tall and he's just about average build . . . and he's wearing heavy clothes, 'cuz of the winter . . . and he has a rifle . . . and he has a scarf around him and . . . his beard has frost on it and kinda whiskers from the cold and . . . and he has kind of a beat-up hat that's tied down around his ears.

DR. F. So then, what happens?

w. Then he . . . he says he'll take me back to town, and I can find my way from town. I just don't know why I'm lost. I shouldn't be lost. I should know this country!

DR. F. Did you get on his horse with him?

w. Yes.

DR. F. How does it feel to be on his horse going back to town?

w. It hurts, because I'm so stiff from being cold. But at least I know I'm not going to get frostbite.

DR. F. You know you're not going to get frostbite?

w. It hurts, and that means I won't get frostbite.

DR. F. All right, move ahead in time to the next significant event . . . one . . . two . . . three.

w. . . . I get back to my cabin and I feel so good to be back . . . it's so strange 'cuz I know . . . I know the country. I couldn't get lost. I've lived here for years and it's just something strange that happened. It feels good . . . everything is back . . . the way it should be.

DR. F. What is the first thing that you do when you get back to your cabin?

W. I look for something to eat, and all I have is some flour and some beans. I still don't have any venison, and I have to go out huntin' again because I still have to get some meat. [His voice heavy with regret.]

DR. F. Did you eat anything in town?

W. Yeah . . . [Smiling.] I had a cup of hot chocolate.

DR. F. How did that taste?

W. It tasted very good. [With obvious relish.]

DR. F. Do you like chocolate?

W. Yeah. I don't hardly get any 'cuz it's hard to get . . . they gave it to me because I was about half-frozen, and it helped.

DR. F. Who gave it to you?

W. Somebody in town, just a nice person.

DR. F. Did you just have one cup?

W. Seems like I had more, I can't really remember. It was good . . . but I have to go out huntin' again.

When we finished following William through other events in his life as Fred, the regression was ended and I brought him out of hypnosis. He frowned and said, "I'm still puzzled about how I could have gotten lost. I was really worried—and cold!" After a few seconds of a thoughtful silence he said, "I know deep inside me now why chocolate has been such an important thing in my life." I informed him, "We're having our first cold snap." Perhaps, in some mysterious mind way, that clicked with Fred's freezing ordeal. In looking back to a year ago, William remembered the same pattern— getting down to 200 and, during a cold spell, surrendering to a craving for chocolate, undermining his diet— and his self-confidence. It was too late to check out (just to satisfy our curiosity) if there were something magical, like Fred weighing exactly 200 pounds at that time. One day we may find out. But for now it's unimportant.

William's inner mind finally agreed that it is willing for him to continue to lose, in a "zigzag" way, until he reaches his goal of 145. We decided to leave well enough alone and work on whatever came up each time, until his goal is reached. We are both happy that as of now he weighs 185 and can resist chocolates to boot.

One day he came in smiling broadly, "Cats have really rough tongues! I let our neighbor's cat lick some butter off the end of my finger. I even enjoyed it. And the best part is I could breathe." He added, "Before, I would have cringed and started wheezing right away if a cat came anywhere near me. So far I haven't had an encounter with chickens. I still think they are stupid!"

CHAPTER SIX

"There Is No Sex For Somebody Like Me"

When I introduced myself to Patricia in the waiting room, I saw a slim, pretty woman in her late twenties, with wavy, light brown hair and frightened hazel eyes. She was casually dressed in a colorful blouse and coordinated slacks. Once in my office, she sat rigidly in the modern reclining chair—a hard thing to do! She gripped the arms of the chair and, with a great deal of obvious discomfort, hesitantly told me what brought her to seek help. "My husband, Mark, and I have been married for eight years. We dated for three years before we got married." Blushing, and tears springing to her eyes, she continued, the words coming slowly, "And we have never had sex." She quickly added that Mark had been away in the service during some of those dating years. With surprising naivete, Patricia went on, "Our marriage seems to be lacking something. We like each other—some of the time. But there must be something more to a relationship." As she unfolded her life, she confessed that she felt "insanely" jealous, without a shred of evidence. Continuing, she revealed a great deal of tension in the relationship and fights that stopped just short of physical violence.

As she talked, she remained almost as tense as she had been during the first moments of our session. At one point she said, "This is murder!" I immediately made the decision to teach her self-hypnosis and let the rest of her story wait. I decided to show her how to relax her body progressively, beginning with closing her eyelids. I usually say, "Let the relaxation from your closed eyelids flow out over your temples like a warm, relaxing liquid." I took one look at her tightly squeezed eyelids and made a quick decision to avoid the word "relaxation," at least initially. After she concentrated on her breathing for several minutes, I noticed the tension begin to yield slowly, but not much. Her hands remained crushed between her knees during the ten minutes or so of the "relaxation" technique. By the end of those ten minutes, I knew I had my work cut out for me in helping Patricia with her uncommon problem.

During the next two visits, using hypnosis, I tried to explore the origins of her fears. Even though she faithfully used the relaxation tape that I had made for her twice a day, there was no budging her defenses against slipping into a deeper trance. Her fingers did not lift to my suggestions, so I could not use my usual questioning techniques. When I asked her to answer verbally, we got nowhere. Nothing she said shed any light on the problem—certainly not enough to explain her overwhelming anxiety about sex.

I set up an appointment with Mark, and several days later he came in alone. He was a handsome, trim young man in his early thirties and was dressed meticulously in colors that complemented his rich brown hair. During our first meeting, he was even more outwardly anxious than his wife had been. In fact, the interview could not have proceeded without distressing him unmercifully. So, then and there, within the first five minutes, I taught him self-relaxation! After that, he smiled weakly at me and his whole body hesitantly eased into the chair. His face remained red and his voice trembled as he told me about their life together. "Nothing works! No matter what I try with Patricia, she sooner or later, and it's usually sooner, says no!" He felt tremendously frustrated and furious. He said, "It seems to me that she feels sex is dirty. It is embarrassing for her to get even a little excited—then she switches off." He blamed himself, feeling that maybe he was doing something wrong. He had tried everything he could think of, including futile attempts to force her.

He felt they had a good marriage, since they cared about each other. But he was totally exasperated because they could not talk about sex—"our big problem." He realized they should have gotten help earlier. He admitted, "I was too macho to expose the problem to anyone, and Patricia was terrified of talking about sex with a therapist. In fact, her doctor had to push her into calling you when he realized how nervous she is."

They began to attend our sessions together. Week after week they made slow progress practicing the various assignments I gave them to help them enjoy each other. At first, they just massaged one another with oils in front of the fire (Patricia could not relax enough in bed) and took showers together. Gradually, in the months that followed, Patricia began to enjoy herself— just a little more, without embarrassment.

However, a pattern emerged. Each week, despite my instructions, their "getting together" would only take place on Saturdays and Sundays. For years Patricia fell asleep—"exhausted"—on the couch after dinner each night as they watched TV together. Now they both questioned whether she was avoiding sex on those days—and, if so, why?

One day they came in smiling broadly and happily presented me with a big bouquet of golden chrysanthemums. I knew in a flash that they had won their first small victory. They had had intercourse for the first time in eleven years! We sat down and they shared the good news with me. A few minutes later, Mark playfully demonstrated Patricia's grimaces during the sex act and we all laughed good-naturedly. She admitted she had made up her mind, "It was now or never," and tried to relax enough to permit penetration. She was so tight he almost gave up, but finally it happened.

Several weeks later, after more sexual counseling, I asked Patricia to start coming in for hypnoanalysis.

Because of her trust in me and general loosening up, she was now an excellent hypnotic subject. She slipped into a deep trance readily and established strong finger signals. Through these signals, her inner mind made it clear that the causes of her problem were deeply hidden from her conscious mind. The roots were not from this lifetime but from previous ones. It had taken us nine

101

months to begin to get some real understanding of the origins of her crippling fears!

I regressed her to "an event a long time ago" that had to do with her problem. Her voice changed considerably, becoming very self-assured and clipped.

P. I feel the sun—it's very hot.

DR. F. What do you see?

P. I see sand and water. It's the sea. It's very blue and clear . . . it's warm.

DR. F. Do you see any people?

P. No, I don't. Just open beaches.

DR. F. Are there many waves?

P. No, it's very tranquil.

DR. F. Now become aware of yourself and tell me what you're wearing and describe yourself.

P. I'm very tall, I'm slim, I'm tan . . . I don't like being here. I feel . . . it's just bothering me to be here.

DR. F. This is not your own country?

P. Yes, it is, because I'm very comfortable. It's my place, where I belong.

DR. F. What is the name of your country?

P. [Surprised.] Kauai? . . . Kauai.

DR. F. What year is it?

P. The Year . . . of the Moon.

DR. F. But you don't want to be here? . . . You don't want to be here at this moment, is that it? Something's happening or going to happen?

P. That might be it.

DR. F. What is your name?

P. . . . I think . . . Alena.

DR. F. What are you wearing, Alena?

P. A dress . . . I think it's blue and white.

DR. F. Do you have many dresses?

P. Oh . . . yes, I have . . . I have some.

DR. F. What do you usually wear?

P. I wear a dress or . . . or just a skirt.

DR. F. And with this skirt, what would you wear?

P. Flowers.

DR. F. Do you wear any blouse or do you just go nude on top?

P. No top.

DR. F. Where did you get the material for this dress?

P. Some sailors gave it to my father . . . he is the chief.

DR. F. And what is your father's name?

P. [Silence.]

DR. F. All right. I'd like you to go to an occasion in which you hear someone addressing your father, at the count of three. One . . . two . . . three.

P. I see men and women standing around. My father is speaking to them and they're bowing and . . . and I'm just standing there listening.

DR. F. What is he speaking to them about?

F. Food, I believe.

DR. F. What is it about food that he's saying?

P. That we don't have enough food.

DR. F. How are you feeling right now?

P. Bored.

DR. F. And just listen to what they call your father. Hear his name being spoken.

P. Tubo comes to mind.

DR. F. All right, go back to the beach where you were before. One . . . two . . . three.

P. I seem to be looking around. I think I'm waiting . . . waiting for someone and he isn't coming . . . I'm feeling very impatient. [Arrogantly.]

DR. F. Whom are you waiting for?

P. My lover. He's supposed to be coming.

DR. F. What is his name?

P. Hmmm . . . Estin comes to mind. It's a pretty name. I like his name.

DR. F. Where is he coming from?

P. Another town.

DR. F. How is he coming?

P. He's coming on a horse. [I remembered reading somewhere that horses were first brought to the Hawaiian Islands around the turn of the nineteenth century.]

DR. F. Now what is happening?

P. I see him coming. I don't know why I had him come. I don't really like him, but I need him. He's . . .

103

he's very handsome, but he thinks too much of himself . . . and not enough of me.

DR. F. Have you been lovers for a long time?

P. Seems like it. Too long, I think, for me. He really makes me mad. [Said petulantly.]

DR. F. What is it about him that makes you mad?

P. Because he's . . . he's interested in other women besides me. [Long pause.]

DR. F. Now what is happening?

P. We're lying on the sand . . . we're having intercourse. He really pleases me that way, but I don't . . . other ways he doesn't.

DR. F. Just enjoy that feeling. Get in touch with your responsiveness.

P. I'm very responsive. I always have been, ever since I can remember.

DR. F. Just with him or with others, too?

P. I think there's been others, too. It always has seemed so good to me.

DR. F. You've always been able to express your sexuality fully, is that what you're saying? To be able to experience orgasms and so forth?

P. I think so. He really gives me a lot of pleasure and Estin seems to get a lot of pleasure, so it must be right.

DR. F. Do you feel okay about having intercourse with him and with others?

P. With others, yes . . . with him, no. He's . . . he's so conceited. He loves himself, he doesn't love me. [With a matter-of-fact tone of voice.]

DR. F. Have the others loved you?

P. Yes . . . but I didn't love them. It was okay, then.

DR. F. What's happening now?

P. Estin's leaving . . . I'm feeling ashamed.

DR. F. Why is that?

P. Because he just . . . he enjoys me, and then he leaves. He doesn't talk to me—he doesn't know me. He doesn't like me particularly, but he enjoys . . . he enjoys what we do, as I do. I want him to enjoy me, not just . . . not just the sex.

DR. F. Do you want to see him again?

P. Yes and no. Same old thing . . . I don't like me this way. He doesn't force himself on me. I ask for it.

DR. F. But you're not happy with the situation, are you?

P. If I didn't enjoy the sex so much, it would be much easier, but it's so nice . . . especially with him.

DR. F. Is he an especially good lover?

P. Yes, very good. He's very tender that way, but other ways . . .

DR. F. Okay now, I'm going to ask your inner mind to choose the next important occasion. One . . . two . . . three.

P. I'm feeling like I should just turn myself off. That will show him! That will really show him! Then he won't enjoy it, then he'll want me, only I won't need him because I won't need that anymore. That'll show him!

DR. F. Do you think you can do that? Turn yourself off?

P. Sure. I can do anything. [Her voice full of confidence, and arrogance.]

DR. F. All right, now I'd like you to move ahead in time and let's see if you did turn yourself off. One . . . two . . . three.

P. I think I did. He came again, later. And he hit me because I didn't want to be with him. I showed him . . . I made him mad.

DR. F. How did you show him?

P. I wouldn't have sex with him.

DR. F. What happened?

P. I just led him on and wouldn't let him come into me at the last minute.

DR. F. How did you feel when you did that?

P. I didn't feel very good myself, but he didn't feel very good either—so that made it okay.

DR. F. Now I'd like you to move forward in time again to another very important event. One . . . two . . . three. What's happening to you?

P. I'm sitting underneath a palm tree . . .

DR. F. Can you tell me more?

P. Hmm . . . feeling kind of . . . depressed.

DR. F. Why is that?

P. Oh . . . I just, hmm . . . don't enjoy . . . sex anymore. The others don't fulfill me like Estin. They

105

seem to . . . they're not . . . there's not the passion there. Ah . . . they're all right but you know . . . it's just . . . it's not the same.

DR. F. You're not getting anything out of it, is that what you're saying?

P. Not much. Some, but not nearly the way it was with Estin.

DR. F. Is Estin still in your life?

P. No.

DR. F. What happened?

P. Well . . . he left and it's just . . . it's not as good.

DR. F. Can you tell me more about that?

P. I just . . . I don't—I just don't get the same feeling.

DR. F. Things have really changed that way for you?

P. Um-hmm.

DR. F. And that depressed you?

P. Oh, yes . . . because it doesn't feel good anymore, like it did with him.

DR. F. When you say he left, what do you mean?

P. He left me, I don't know if he left the island. He may still be here, I haven't seen him.

DR. F. Has it been some time since you've seen him?

P. Um-hmm . . . feels like it.

DR. F. And when you're with other men, you just don't enjoy sex?

P. It's not—not the same, not the same feeling. It's . . . just . . . not like it was with him.

DR. F. Before you met him, you were able to enjoy other men sexually?

P. I thought I was, but then . . . when we had sex . . . I knew I had been missing . . . [Long pause.]

DR. F. Can you tell me some more about yourself, how you're feeling?

P. [Words coming slowly.] Oh . . . I feel angry because he left and . . . just . . . bored.

DR. F. What is your life like now? How do you spend your days?

P. Oh . . . I get up and . . . eat some fruit and . . . swim . . . the water's good for swimming, and just . . . lie around. I don't . . . I don't do work.

DR. F. Do you have any interests? Do you like to paint, or sing, or play any musical instruments?

P. No. I like to . . . to walk in the . . . the hills and take . . . take lunch. I do . . . I do have a . . . a wooden tube and it makes . . . makes sounds. I like that. I go alone and sit up on the hill and look over . . . the water. I took Estin there.

DR. F. Sounds like a beautiful spot.

P. Um-hmm.

DR. F. Have you always lived on this one island?

P. Um-hmm.

DR. F. Can you tell me more about the island?

P. Hmm . . . men are fishing every day. They bring us fish, food. Women are making . . . making food from the fish . . . and the chief is umm . . . he's troubled.

DR. F. Why is he troubled?

P. I think one of the other islands is going to . . . to make war.

DR. F. Do you know how to write and do you read?

P. Hmm . . . no.

DR. F. You've never been to school. You don't have schools?

P. No. We have no schools . . . no.

DR. F. Who is in your family?

P. I think I have . . . three sisters. They're gooses . . . they're . . . they're gooses, they're . . .

DR. F. They're gooses?

P. They're . . . silly.

DR. F. Are they younger than you?

P. Yes.

DR. F. I'm going to ask your inner mind to take you to an event in your home so that you can get in touch with that. One . . . two . . . three. What are you doing now?

P. Hmm . . . I'm sitting on the . . . sitting on the ground.

DR. F. Where are you?

P. Inside a hut.

DR. F. Whose hut is it?

107

P. I think it's my hut.

DR. F. Is it your own hut or do you share it with some other members of your family?

P. It's . . . it's my own.

DR. F. Can you tell me what you have in it? Can you describe it to me?

P. Umm . . . mats for lying down . . . pot.

DR. F. What is that for?

P. Hmm . . . I think it's for food . . . and it's . . . the sun comes in and it's warm, nice.

DR. F. Do you like your hut?

P. Um-hmm.

DR. F. Do you see any of your family?

P. I can see my father standing on the beach . . . with his . . . with his—belly hanging out. [Laughs softly.]

DR. F. What do you think of that scene?

P. Oh . . . hmm. He's just funny.

DR. F. What do you mean?

P. He's—he's fat. He's got a big belly.

DR. F. Is your mother fat, too?

P. Hmm . . .

DR. F. Can you see her?

P. No.

DR. F. Can you see any of your sisters?

P. Just—just ah . . . my father standing on the beach.

DR. F. Okay, now I'm going to ask your inner mind to take you to an occasion you will be with your whole family. One . . . two . . . three. Whatever comes to mind.

P. Oh, we're eating, all of us, my three sisters and father.

DR. F. Anybody else?

P. Mmm . . .I think my uncle is there too.

DR. F. Where's your mother?

P. Hmm . . . I don't know. [Sounding puzzled.]

DR. F. Does she usually eat with you?

P. She's—I don't . . . I don't know of her.

DR. F. But you live with your father and three sisters?

P. Um-hmm.

DR. F. Is there just one chief on the island?

P. Um-hmm.

DR. F. And what are you eating?

P. Some . . . some fruits and some fish and some . . . some smashed fish and vegetable root.

DR. F. Who prepares the food?

P. Some of the women on the island.

DR. F. Okay now, move forward in time to another very significant event. One . . . two . . . three.

P. [Long pause.] I think I'm . . . dying . . . I'm feeling foolish about myself for what I did. [Her voice heavy and sad.]

DR. F. What is it you did?

P. I cut myself off. I . . . I made myself stop enjoying and that was foolish of me, and now it's over, and what can I do? I can't enjoy. That was really foolish of me . . . like that.

DR. F. You feel you made a really bad choice, a bad mistake?

P. I think I did.

DR. F. Are you an old lady now, Alena?

P. I don't think so . . . I don't think I'm very old, but . . . I am getting ready to die.

DR. F. How do you know that?

P. I don't know.

DR. F. What else are you aware of?

P. I feel like I want Estin again. It's been . . . it's been many years since I've seen him . . . but I still want him in the same old way. [Tears welling up.] I wish I hadn't done that to him. A lot of wasted years.

DR. F. Have you ever married and had children?

P. No, I don't think so.

DR. F. Are you sick now? Is that why you're dying?

P. I don't feel sick.

DR. F. Now, go right up to the moment of your death. Get in touch with what it is that's causing your death and how it feels to die. One . . . two . . . three. And what are you experiencing?

P. I'm lying there.

DR. F. Is there anyone with you?

P. There seem to be a lot of people gathered around. [Calmly and quietly.] I don't feel any pain but I know I'm going to die.

DR. F. Where are you? Are you in your own home, or . . . ?

P. I'm outside. I think they're going to kill me.

DR. F. They're going to kill you?

P. I think so. I think it's . . . I think it's a sacrifice. I think that's what it is and I . . . don't care. Doesn't make any difference to me that I'm going to die.

DR. F. How are they going to kill you?

P. I think they throw me into a mountain. A volcano? I don't know.

DR. F. How do you get up there?

P. I think it's . . . they carried me up there on a platform in my blue and white dress and then they just throw me in, I think.

DR. F. Is this the custom where you live?

P. I believe it is.

DR. F. At the count of three, you'll know exactly where you are and why it is the custom, and under what circumstances one is chosen. One . . . two . . . three.

P. I'm the chief's daughter and there's been . . . it's been a bad year for crops, no water and the only way to appease the gods is to . . . to sacrifice me and I know that.

While she was still under hypnosis, I agreed with Patricia that she had made a mistake in "turning herself off" and gave her suggestions to give herself permission to recapture the sexual responsiveness she so naturally felt in that lifetime. Her inner mind signaled agreement.

She was brought out of hypnosis and we talked about her first experience as "someone else."

DR. F. Do you feel you're back here now?

P. Yeah. [Laughing.]

DR. F. Do you feel like you're a very different person than you were?

P. Yeah. Well, yes and no. I felt very regal, you know, just . . .

DR. F. You were acting it. You had a kind of arrogant way about you.

P. I could tell, I could tell. I felt, "Gee, this is a differ-

110

ent me." I'm not, you know, like that. Maybe I am, but I'm not. [Laughing.] I had such a, sort of passé attitude about my other lovers, you know, who cares? No matter what they felt for me. I just, you know . . . it's wild.

DR. F. Did you feel like you were very emotionally involved with Estin even though it wasn't a good relationship?

P. I felt like I was involved with him, but he wasn't with me.

DR. F. But you didn't like him?

P. I didn't *like* him, but I did, sort of. I was . . . maybe I didn't like him because he didn't like me, but I really did, you know, I really . . . I really wanted him.

DR. F. You really wanted something more from him. So you decided that you didn't like him when actually you did.

P. Yes, I think that's it.

DR. F. Did that explain to you what happened to you up there in this lifetime? Does that make sense to you?

P. Yes. It does. It really kind of explains why I won't let myself go. It's funny, at times during it, I was thinking, oh, this is just fantasy, you know, I'm making the whole stupid thing up! But then I get sort of flashes of, like the scenes, you know, that . . .

DR. F. Now with the sacrifice, were you up at the top of the mountain when you were describing that?

P. Well, when I was first describing it, I was down below, because I just saw myself lying on a slab, but then I was up at the top of the mountain, and I think they threw me in.

DR. F. Did you see yourself being thrown in?

P. No.

DR. F. But you weren't afraid?

P. No, not a bit. It was just very . . . you know . . . so what!

DR. F. How did you react to my questions?

P. I thought, who is that asking *me* all these questions? I felt very arrogant and bothered.

In the first minutes of our next meeting, Patricia regaled me with the details of Mark's reactions to his wife having been a Hawaiian princess. First, he experienced total shock—then disbelief—and finally, intrigued, he began to ask a thousand questions. Was he Estin? "I don't feel you were," Patricia answered. Mark was momentarily jealous. But her sexual reaction delighted them both. "I told Mark I felt so sexy I couldn't believe it." She noticed feelings in her body that were stronger than any she had ever experienced before (in this lifetime!). She wanted to make love then and there—but Mark had just come down with a case of intestinal flu, so *he* was out of commission for a few days. Then she came down with it. Between sessions with me, they had made love only once. "But what a change!" she exclaimed. "I could feel all those lovely feelings, just as I had as Alena—no, not quite that strong—but a hundred times better than before." She was obviously encouraged and her whole face was aglow.

After a moment, she said, "An odd thing happened. I realized I felt guilty." She contrasted this with the earlier feelings of disgust, anger and anxiety she had experienced during the years of their marriage. Now, feeling less anxious, she was sensing that she was doing something wrong—yet she knew, intellectually, that it wasn't wrong. She was puzzled.

I hypnotized her and asked her inner mind if something had happened to make her feel guilty. Within minutes she found herself in "another place, at another time, as another person."

P. I'm sitting underneath a tree . . . I think it's an apple tree . . . green grass.

DR. F. Describe yourself and your surroundings.

P. I think I'm twelve—and I have braids and I'm just sitting there on this mountaintop—looking at . . . down at the valley and the green . . . it's really lush and pretty . . . it's crisp . . . I like being here.

DR. F. I'd like you to describe what you're wearing and know about yourself. Know your name.

P. Kim comes to mind . . . Kimberly Bjorg. Fair-

112

skinned. I think I'm wearing a blue apron—blue checkered apron. I'm sitting underneath an apple tree.

DR. F. Kim, why are you there?

P. Just being peaceful and enjoying the spring day. [Smiling.] It's awfully nice out.

DR. F. Where do you live, Kim?

P. Up . . . up the hill.

DR. F. Who's in your family?

P. Mother and Father and . . . George.

DR. F. Who's George.

P. . . . My brother.

DR. F. Is he older than you or younger?

P. Older.

DR. F. What country do you live in?

P. Sweden? . . . Sweden.

DR. F. What's the name of your town? Do you live near town?

P. No, we live out . . . out in the country.

DR. F. Do you live near a town?

P. Umm . . . it's not very close . . . Knightstown comes to mind.

DR. F. How about describing it to me? Can you see it from where you're sitting?

P. No, it's further than that.

DR. F. What's the year, Kimberly?

P. Hmm.

DR. F. It will come to you on the count of three. One . . . two . . . three.

P. Eighteen something . . . Eighteen twenty-five comes to mind.

DR. F. I'm going to ask your inner mind to move ahead to a very significant event. Something that's important for you to know about. One . . . two . . . three.

P. It's George. He's coming up the hill. [Voice full of excitement.]

DR. F. Are you still sitting under the apple tree?

P. Um-hmm.

DR. F. How do you feel when you see him coming up?

P. Bad. He'll . . . he'll want to . . . play those games

113

again, and I . . . really I don't like it, but . . . he likes, you know . . . he likes them.

DR. F. Can you tell me about these games?

P. [Shyly.] Oh, no.

DR. F. You'd rather not?

P. Yes.

DR. F. You know I'm a doctor—I don't tell anybody anything that you say—and I don't judge you. Maybe that would make it easier for you to tell me.

P. But . . . hmm.

DR. F. You sound a little embarrassed about it—are you?

F. Um-hmm.

DR. F. Has he been wanting you to play these games for a long time?

P. Oh . . . it seems like it.

DR. F. How old were you when he started?

P. Ten.

DR. F. Describe what happens as you see George coming.

P. Oh . . . he's coming up the hill and asks me if I want to play, and I say, "No" . . . but we do it anyway.

DR. F. Can you tell me more about it now?

P. Oh, we kind of touch each other and he makes funny noises and . . . I—I—I enjoy it, but . . . but I . . . but I don't think I should. [She lowers her voice to a whisper.]

DR. F. What makes you think you shouldn't?

P. Well, we're . . . we're brother and sister. I don't think we're supposed to do things like that with each other.

DR. F. Did someone tell you this?

P. I've—I've heard. I know.

DR. F. When he does touch you, how do you feel?

P. Oh . . . oh, it feels—it feels pretty good, but . . . I feel rotten afterwards.

DR. F. You feel really bad about yourself afterwards?

P. I know . . . he talks me into it, but I know that we shouldn't do that.

DR. F. Do you do this in the nude?

P. No, no!

114

DR. F. Do you do anything other than just touching?

P. That's—that's about . . . that's it.

DR. F. Does he ever suggest doing anything more than just touching each other?

P. He hasn't.

DR. F. All right, now just let that memory continue and just describe what happens.

P. Oh, he . . . he's . . . he's leaving and laughing and I'm just sitting there—and thinking that I'm not very smart—not feeling very good.

DR. F. When you say you're not feeling very good, can you tell me what that means to you?

P. In my mind—I'm not happy about me.

DR. F. Now just let that memory fade and concentrate on your breathing again, and I'm going to ask your inner mind to take you to another very important event. One . . . two . . . three.

P. George is getting married. Now we won't have those games . . . and I really feel bad, but I'm going to miss it. I almost feel jealous of his wife.

DR. F. You've come to accept these games and like them?

P. Yes.

DR. F. How old are you now?

P. Fifteen.

DR. F. How old is George?

P. Twenty.

DR. F. Tell me what's happened in these three years from the time you were twelve sitting under that apple tree until now, as far as these games are concerned.

P. Well, we do more than just . . . did more than just touch.

DR. F. You're biting your lip. Why are you doing that?

P. Because I don't want to tell you.

DR. F. I'm not going to tell anyone. I'm a doctor and I don't judge you. I'm just here to help, so just tell me whatever you can about what you did and get some of your feelings out. That will be very helpful to you.

P. [Pause.] Oh . . . he . . . he likes to . . . experiment.

115

DR. F. Experiment?

P. Petting . . .

DR. F. [Remembering Patricia's avoidance of sex during the week.] Do you pet with George every day?

P. No.

DR. F. Are there certain days when you don't?

P. He's gone . . . ah . . . two days.

DR. F. And where does he go?

P. To the village.

DR. F. What does he do in the village?

P. He gets food and sees his friends and cuts wood.

DR. F. He cuts wood in the village?

P. I think . . . he brings wood. He brings wood back up.

DR. F. Is it a long way from the village—does it take quite a long time to get there?

P. Hours.

DR. F. So when he goes down on the weekends does he stay overnight there?

P. Yes.

DR. F. What is his custom? When does he leave?

P. Oh . . . Saturday morning—very early.

DR. F. And he comes back when?

P. Sunday evening.

DR. F. How do you feel with him gone?

P. Oh . . . I miss him . . . but in a way I feel relieved, I guess.

DR. F. I know that people can be attracted to each other—and enjoy each other even if they are brother and sister.

P. But, it isn't right.

DR. F. Our bodies don't know that, it's our minds—because that's what we've been taught, because that's the way our society thinks. Do you understand what I'm saying to you?

P. Yes.

DR. F. So will you tell me some more now about what you've experienced together?

P. We . . . umm . . . we . . . we had sex together.

DR. F. And how was that for you. How did that feel to you?

116

P. Umm . . . felt good. [Lowering her voice.]

DR. F. Is this something that happened frequently?

P. Yes . . . except on Saturdays and Sundays.

DR. F. When you had sex with him, were you able to feel excited feelings and feel something that felt like a climax?

P. [Pause.]

DR. F. Do you know what I mean by that word?

P. Yeah . . . No, I don't think so.

DR. F. But, you did enjoy it?

P. Yes.

DR. F. When was the last time that you had sex?

P. Oh, about . . . a week ago and then he said that we couldn't do it anymore, because he's getting married.

DR. F. What did you say to that?

P. I said "Okay." What could I say?

DR. F. Did anyone ever find out about your games?

P. No . . . not—not that I know of.

DR. F. Do you know how babies are conceived?

P. Yes.

DR. F. Do you worry about that?

P. No.

DR. F. And now I'd like you to just let go of that memory and concentrate on your breathing and I want to ask your inner mind to move ahead to the next important event—something that you need to know about. One . . . two . . . three.

P. [Pause.]

DR. F. What are you experiencing?

P. I think I'm pregnant. [Her chin quivering.]

DR. F. What makes you think that, Kim?

P. I don't know.

DR. F. It's going to become clearer and clearer on the count of three. One . . . two . . . three. And where are you and what's happening?

P. I'm sitting at the kitchen table—and my mother and father are having a fight.

DR. F. What are they fighting about?

P. It's about me.

DR. F. Tell me more.

117

P. I am . . . I *am* pregnant—going to have a baby. I'm not married.

DR. F. Do they know that you're pregnant?

P. Yes.

DR. F. And how do they feel about it?

P. They're angry, because I'm not married—but they don't—they don't know . . . who . . . the father is.

DR. F. You haven't told them?

P. No. Can't. [About to cry.]

DR. F. Are they trying to make you tell them?

P. Yes.

DR. F. And what are they fighting about?

P. They're arguing with each other—but they're very angry with me.

DR. F. And how do you feel?

P. Very badly—very embarrassed, just . . . confused.

DR. F. How do you know you're pregnant?

P. My stomach's very big.

DR. F. Have you been to see the doctor yet?

P. No.

DR. F. And you know who the father is? Does he know about it yet?

P. No, I can't tell him.

DR. F. Why is that?

P. Because . . . it's . . . it's George.

DR. F. Does George ever come to visit your home?

P. Yes.

DR. F. Can't he see that you're pregnant?

P. He doesn't know it's . . . it's with him. He teases me. [Voice brimming with anger.]

DR. F. What does he say to you?

P. Oh, he laughs because I'm pregnant.

DR. F. And you're protecting him?

P. Well, I just . . . I'm not doing it for that—for him. I'm doing it for me, I'm so ashamed of myself. I couldn't tell anybody.

DR. F. I'm going to ask your inner mind to take you to the next important event on the count of three. One . . . two . . . three.

P. [Pause.]

118

DR. F. What are you experiencing, Kim?

P. Well, I can't stay here. [Her voice heavy with resignation.]

DR. F. Where are you now?

P. I'm on the mountain top.

DR. F. Why is it you can't stay there?

P. Because I can't stay here and have this baby. I think . . . I think I'm going to jump because I can't . . . can't have this baby! [Sounding panicky.]

DR. F. Where are you going to jump?

P. Off the mountain, then . . . then everything will be solved.

DR. F. Have you given this a lot of thought?

P. No, but I have to do . . . I hate myself for what I did . . . and I don't want the baby. It's just not real to me. I can't . . . I can't face George. I can't face Mother and Father . . . I have to do something. I feel so . . . so bad, and I'm going to . . . it'll be better. At least I won't have . . . explain to them.

DR. F. Just describe what you do next.

P. [Pause.]

DR. F. Tell me what you're experiencing.

P. [Pause.]

DR. F. Tell me what you see or what you're experiencing.

P. I jumped . . . but I'm still . . . I'm still alive. I can feel myself falling. I don't . . . hmm.

DR. F. Where are you now?

P. [Pause.]

DR. F. What are you experiencing now?

P. Nothing. I feel like I'm floating. I'm glad it's over.

I brought Patricia back to the present and explained under hypnosis that perhaps her sexual attraction to her brother had been allowed to reach her conscious mind because in her prior incarnation (which probably ended very soon before the lifetime as Kim) she had been a Hawaiian princess. Members of the royal family were allowed to have sexual relations with each other and possibly she had carried over, at least to some degree, enough of that permissiveness so that it overrode the

119

taboo against incest. She agreed readily and her face and body relaxed—her expression was one of immense relief. Then I asked her if George was anyone she knew in this lifetime. She answered slowly that he was Mark.

During our next session, Patricia smiled triumphantly as she strolled into my office. As soon as she took off her coat and settled herself in her chair, she said, "Mark and I are really enjoying getting together." In a rush of words, she exclaimed, "We have had sex during the week for the first time—and I enjoyed it!" With amazement in her voice, she said, "I can feel myself getting more excited each time we make love." I asked her, "Are you still aware of the guilty feeling you mentioned last time?" "It's gone. No guilt at all. Just plain enjoyment," she said with a big smile.

Because she was still not experiencing a climax, I put her into a trance and asked if there were anything at a subconscious level that was keeping her from fully enjoying sex. Her "yes" finger lifted. Again her inner mind signaled that we needed to investigate a previous lifetime. I suggested that her subconscious mind take her to "an event that will be very helpful for you to understand—that has to do with your sexuality." At the count of ten, she found herself "just looking, feeling sort of helpless," standing on a dirt road in the middle of Larzo, a town near Barcelona. The year was 1901.

P. There is no . . . there is no sex for somebody like me . . . nobody would want me. [Her voice trembling with emotion.]

DR. F. Why do you say that?

P. Look. [Gesturing.] I'm fat. Who'd want all that? Too many tortillas.

DR. F. How long have you been fat?

P. I can't remember being skinny.

DR. F. What is your name?

P. Tia.

DR. F. Why do they call you Tia? Any special reason? [Remembering from college Spanish that "tia" means "aunt."]

P. It's what my . . . it's what my nephew calls me. Oh, it just was cute . . . so it stuck.

DR. F. What is your real name?

P. Margarita.

DR. F. And how old are you?

P. I'm thirty.

DR. F. Are you married?

P. No.

DR. F. Do you have any idea why it is that you eat so much?

P. It's safer that way.

DR. F. What do you mean, "safer"?

P. When I'm fat, people can't hurt me.

DR. F. What do you mean?

P. Well, no one would think of . . . no man would think of loving me, so I'm not . . . being's I'm not available or I'm fat, nobody can . . . nobody would even try to . . . to come close to me . . . and so, being as they all feel that way, then I can't get hurt.

DR. F. Were you ever hurt by someone?

P. No.

DR. P. What makes you so afraid of being hurt?

P. Oh . . . I've seen other people.

DR. F. Who?

P. Well . . . my mother.

DR. F. What happened to your mother?

P. My father left her for . . . for someone else that was young and pretty and he laughed at her and told her she was old and ugly and didn't want her anymore.

DR. F. Did you hear that happen?

P. Yes.

DR. F. How old were you when that happened?

P. Seven.

DR. F. How did you feel, Tia?

P. I felt the shame for her.

DR. F. And how did you feel about yourself?

P. I felt I would never, never let that happen to me.

Out of the trance, Patricia shook her head in bewilderment. "Wow! Was that me, too?" she asked. "She

121

felt so unwanted—so afraid of being hurt." She admitted that down deep she had many of the same fears, but fortunately not so strongly.

The next week, Patricia reported, "I'm feeling more and more pleasure when Mark and I have intercourse. I'm more relaxed and I even find myself looking forward to making love. I have never before looked *forward* to it." When I questioned her more closely, she revealed with a tone of bewilderment and frustration, "I'm aware now of tightening up. I become quite anxious just as Mark is about to penetrate." She added quickly, "But I'm really happy, because sex is becoming so enjoyable. What a change!"

The image of an onion popped into my mind—as soon as we peel off one layer, we are faced with another!

Almost predictably, under hypnosis, Patricia's subconscious mind indicated that there was another past lifetime experience that was obstructing the free flow of her sexual expression.

I regressed her and she slowly and sadly said:

P. I'm sitting on a bench . . . looking at the street.
DR. F. And what does the street look like?
P. It's white . . . the buildings are white . . . everything's white.
DR. F. What are you doing on this bench? Why are you sitting there?
P. Waiting for a bus.
DR. F. Where are you?
P. Egypt.
DR. F. And just let me know what happens, as you let time roll forward.
P. [Her chin quivering.] Hmm . . . I'm nervous about something.
DR. F. I'm going to count from one to three and on the count of three you'll know why you're nervous. One . . . two . . . three.
P. I'm . . . I'm going to a new place . . . I can't be here anymore. [Said with regret.]

122

DR. F. Why is that?

P. . . . I'm . . . I'm of age and I have to leave.

DR. F. Where are you going?

P. To another town.

DR. F. Are you there by yourself?

P. I'm sitting on the bench alone . . .

DR. F. All right, and now I'd like you to move forward in time to a time when something significant happens at the count of three. One . . . two . . . three. What are you experiencing now?

P. I don't want to go.

DR. F. Why is that?

P. I'm afraid. [Her voice quavering.]

DR. F. What are you afraid of?

P. I don't know . . . what will be in the new town.

DR. F. Are you going to stay with people you know?

P. No.

DR. F. Where will you be staying?

P. I don't know.

DR. F. You mean you're just going to that town and then you'll have to find your own way once you get there?

P. Um-hmm.

DR. F. How old are you?

P. Oh . . . umm . . . sixteen.

DR. F. What is your name?

P. Hmmm . . .

DR. F. Whatever comes to mind.

P. [Pause.]

DR. F. Did something occur to you?

P. No.

DR. F. I'm going to ask you to move forward in time to the time that you arrive in this other town. One . . . two . . . three.

P. I'm . . . I'm in the new town. I feel . . . completely alone. I don't know where to go . . . just . . . lost. [Sadly.]

DR. F. So you feel completely alone?

P. Um-hmm.

DR. F. What will you do?

P. I don't know.

DR. F. Do you have any money?

123

P. Hmm . . . I have some money.

DR. F. What will you do?

P. I've been . . . I've been a waitress . . . ah . . . but I don't know right now . . . what I'll do.

DR. F. Why are you sent away? You said you couldn't stay because you are of age. Is that the custom for people to be sent away?

P. But that's what they told me.

DR. F. Who told you that?

P. My mother? . . . My mother told me that.

DR. F. Why is it your parents sent you away?

P. I think my father liked me too much and my mother . . . my mother sent me away because of the situation.

DR. F. When you say your father liked you too much, can you tell me more about that?

P. He wanted to get too friendly with me. My mother got very jealous.

DR. F. Were you aware of this?

P. Well, I liked my father . . . I didn't think it was so, but my mother told me it was so.

DR. F. What did your mother say to you?

P. She said that I was . . . I was too pretty—that my father liked me more than her and that I had to go.

DR. F. How do you feel about your mother doing that?

P. I think she was wrong, but I have to obey her.

DR. F. What is the name of the town that you're in?

P. Zat.

DR. F. What is the year?

P. What is a "year"?

DR. F. No. what year is it? What is the date?

P. [Pause.]

DR. F. It doesn't matter if you don't know. Tell me what you're wearing.

P. It's . . . a blue . . . material . . . it's wrapped around me.

DR. F. Is it a heavy material or a light material?

P. It's very light.

DR. F. What color blue is it?

P. Oh . . . like the sky. It's a pretty dress. It's my best.

DR. F. What do you have on your feet?

124

P. Nothing.

DR. F. Do you have anything on your head?

P. I have a blue spot.

DR. F. A blue what?

P. A blue spot.

DR. F. What is that?

P. It's . . . it's a fine paint, I put on my forehead.

DR. F. Where do you put it on your forehead?

P. In the center.

DR. F. What . . .

P. It's above on my forehead.

DR. F. Is that the custom?

P. Yes.

DR. F. Do you wear any other makeup?

P. No, it's not allowed.

DR. F. Is the blue spot considered make-up?

P. It's more like an adornment. It's more like a . . . it's not like a make-up, no.

DR. F. Do you put it on every day, or how often do you put it on?

P. Every day.

DR. F. Tell me what you look like.

P. I'm . . . short, slim . . . and my hair is black—and long.

DR. F. How do you wear it?

P. Pulled—tight and in a knot behind my head.

DR. F. What do they call you? What's your name?

P. Meteus.

DR. F. Do you have another name?

P. Seat . . . that's my father's name.

DR. F. All right now, move forward in time at the count of three to some important event. One . . . two . . . three.

P. I found a place to stay.

DR. F. What is it like?

P. It's . . . it's like a hotel. It's white . . . white floors. The room is stark.

DR. F. What's in the room?

P. A cot and . . . and . . . I think there's a chair.

DR. F. Are there any pictures on the wall?

P. No, it's plain—no pictures.

125

DR. F. Have you stayed overnight yet?

P. No, it's my first day.

DR. F. What are you planning to do now?

P. Look for something to do. I don't have enough money to stay here very long. I have to have more money.

DR. F. Is this the first you've been away from home?

P. Yes, it is. [Becoming frightened.]

DR. F. What was the bus ride like?

P. I . . . I don't know. I . . . my thoughts were filled with—fear of—"What am I going to do."

DR. F. Was it a long trip?

P. No.

DR. F. How far away from your home are you?

P. Oh . . . only hours.

DR. F. All right, now just let time move forward to another important event at the count of three. One . . . two . . . three.

P. Hmm . . . there's a . . . a man at my door. [Her whole body trembling.]

DR. F. Where are you?

P. I'm in my room.

DR. F. What is he doing at your door?

P. I don't know.

DR. F. Is he knocking on your door or is the door open?

P. Hmm . . . he's just there.

DR. F. What does he look like?

P. I think he's big, I don't know. I can't see him.

DR. F. Why is that?

P. Because the door is closed.

DR. F. How do you know he's there?

P. I can hear him.

DR. F. What is he doing?

P. I think he's waiting for me to open the door.

DR. F. Did he call to you or knock on the door?

P. Hmmm . . . he said something.

DR. F. Do you remember what it was?

P. He wants me to open the door.

DR. F. How do you feel?

P. I don't want to open the door. [Said with firm determination.]

126

DR. F. Why is that?

P. Because I don't know him.

DR. F. And then what happens?

P. He goes away.

DR. F. Do you have a lock on the door?

P. Yes, or else he would have come in.

DR. F. He tried to open the door?

P. Yes.

DR. F. How do you feel?

P. I feel like I don't want to be here.

DR. F. Where do you want to be?

P. Back home.

DR. F. Move forward in time to the next important event at the count of three. One . . . two . . . three.

P. I'm finding it hard to . . . to find something to do.

DR. F. You don't have work yet?

P. No.

DR. F. What have you tried so far?

P. Just what I know. Umm . . . being . . . umm . . . a waitress in some of the small—restaurants.

DR. F. And they don't need help?

P. No.

DR. F. What will you do?

P. I don't know.

DR. F. Now just move forward to the next important event at the count of three. One . . . two . . . three.

P. I'm back in my room—and . . . the feeling of loneliness . . . and he's at my door again.

DR. F. Do you know who he is? Have you seen him?

P. I think he's the owner of the inn.

DR. F. What is he doing at your door?

P. He wants to come in.

DR. F. What does he want?

P. Ohh . . . to have sex.

DR. F. How do you know this?

P. I just know it.

DR. F. How do you feel about that?

P. I feel like I don't want to.

DR. F. Have you ever had sex with anyone?

127

P. No.

DR. F. What is he like—this owner of the inn?

P. He's big . . . and—ugly.

DR. F. Does he live there in the inn?

P. Yes.

DR. F. What's happening now?

P. Hmmm . . . he got in my room. [Becoming terrified.]

DR. F. He's in your room now?

P. Yes.

DR. F. How did that happen?

P. He got in. I don't know. [Panicky now.]

DR. F. Where are you?

P. Umm . . . we're on the bed, the cot.

DR. F. And what's happening?

P. He's—forcing me . . . to have sex with him. [Breathing hard.]

DR. F. How do you feel?

P. Helpless . . . scared.

DR. F. What's he doing at this moment?

P. Oh, he's just . . . kissing and pulling and . . . it's ugly. [Said with disgust.]

DR. F. Okay, just move forward in time to the next important event. One . . . two . . . three.

P. Humph!

DR. F. What?

P. Oh, he . . . after he was through with me, he laughed at me. [Short laugh.]

DR. F. He laughed at you?

P. Yes.

DR. F. Did he say anything?

P. He said that—I was a virgin.

DR. F. How did you feel?

P. Hopeless.

DR. F. How was it, having sex with him?

P. [Short laugh.] Awful.

DR. F. In what way?

P. He was . . . he was . . . very large . . . and I'm very small . . . and it hurt. [She shudders.]

DR. F. And it hurt you?

128

P. Umm-hmm. I just . . . feel like . . . I'd like to kill him!!

DR. F. Stay calm and relaxed and let your inner mind take you now to the next significant event, at the count of three. One . . . two . . . three. What are you experiencing now?

P. Oh, he came back again. [Depressed.]

DR. F. When did he come back?

P. In the morning.

DR. F. Is he there now?

P. Yes. [Trembling.]

DR. F. What is happening now?

P. The same.

DR. F. What do you do?

P. What can I do? [Said with resignation and anger.]

DR. F. And how does it feel this time?

P. The same.

DR. F. Do you struggle with him?

P. I try, but he is . . . he's so big . . . he's a horse! [Squirming.]

DR. F. Are you crying?

P. Yes, and fighting, and . . . but it doesn't do any good.

That same day Meteus left the hotel and by luck found a job as a servant in the home of an older couple. She described her household duties, one of which was going to fetch water on special occasions from a spring in the desert on "beasts" that were "awkward but lovable" (camels?). She married and died at twenty-six during the birth of her first child. It was a hard labor, with only her husband assisting her. After her son was born, she just found herself "drifting away—farther and farther—feeling peace for the first time in years."

Out of the trance she shook her head sadly as she whimpered, "Oh, god, it was—was terrible being raped!" Tears streamed down her face. She sobbed quietly for several minutes. After she regained her composure, I asked her about the other people in the regression. "I sensed that my father in that lifetime was Mark—and the man who raped me was my father-in-law. I've never felt comfortable with him." Even though she felt all of this very strongly, she said, "I'm not totally convinced that it really happened—but why would I concoct such a story?"

The next week Patricia radiated happiness as she reported, "Things are better than ever sexually. I can feel myself getting so passionate. I feel more passion than I ever believed existed." With a note of gravity she added, "I'm sure I was close to an orgasm, but I still couldn't quite make it."

Within minutes, after slipping into a profound trance, her inner mind revealed that there was still another lifetime we needed to understand. This was her fifth in five sessions! Would this be the final obstacle?

Within a few minutes Patricia's voice changed subtly and a "little girl" started timidly to tell her story:

P. I see a . . . an old wooden shack. It's falling apart.

DR. F. What else do you see?

P. I see an old man with a long beard . . . skinny . . .

DR. F. What is he doing?

P. He's . . . mmm . . . he's standing at the door.

DR. F. Who is he?

P. He's my father.

DR. F. Where are you?

P. I'm outside.

DR. F. Tell me about yourself.

P. I'm five.

DR. F. You're five years old? Are you a little girl or a little boy?

P. Girl.

DR. F. What's your name?

P. Becky. [Shyly.]

DR. F. And where do you live, Becky?

P. Arizona.

DR. F. What are you doing?

P. I'm just standing . . . not doing anything.

DR. F. And now I'm going to ask your inner mind to take you forward in time to the time of a significant event—something that will be important for you to

130

know about. One . . . two . . . three. What are you experiencing?

P. Here comes someone on a horse . . . he's tall and has dark hair.

DR. F. Is he a younger man than your father?

P. Um-hmm.

DR. F. Is it someone you know?

P. I don't—I don't know.

DR. F. How old are you now?

P. I'm still . . . I'm still five.

DR. F. Now what's happening?

P. He's . . . he's walking toward me. I feel . . . I'm . . . I'm weak.

DR. F. You're weak?

P. I'm hungry.

DR. F. Why is that?

P. I haven't eaten.

DR. F. Since when?

P. Two days.

DR. F. Why is that?

P. We . . . we don't have food.

DR. F. Whom do you live with?

P. Father.

DR. F. Just your father?

P. Um-hmm.

DR. F. How do you feel as this man walks toward you?

P. I just . . . look at him. I don't feel anything.

DR. F. Is it someone that you know?

P. I've seen him.

DR. F. And now what happens?

P. He picks me up . . . and . . . holds me. I don't know why he does that. [Sounding puzzled.] I don't . . . I don't like him, you know?

DR. F. And now what happens?

P. He's undressing me. [Fearfully.]

DR. F. And where is this happening?

P. Out of doors.

DR. F. Is anyone else there?

P. My father's inside.

DR. F. How do you feel as he's undressing you?

131

P. Confused. Why—why is he doing that? . . . I don't like it. [She covers her eyes with both hands.]

DR. F. And now what is he doing?

P. [Whispering.] He's . . . he's touching me.

DR. F. How do you feel about that?

P. I'm struggling . . . I'm . . . I don't like what he's doing to me. [Voice sounds distressed.]

DR. F. And now what?

P. He puts me down and . . . just looks at me, and then . . . he's going in to talk to Father.

DR. F. Do you have anything on now?

P. No.

DR. F. How do you feel about this?

P. Horrible. [In a small, withdrawn voice.]

DR. F. Are you crying?

P. No.

DR. F. Did you say anything to him?

P. No.

DR. F. Now just move a little forward in time. Now what's happening?

P. He's coming back out.

DR. F. Is he coming out alone?

P. Yes.

DR. F. And where are you now?

P. I'm standing alongside of the house. I don't want him to see me. [Whispered.]

DR. F. Did you get dressed?

P. Yes . . . he's leaving.

DR. F. And now what are you doing?

P. I'm going in the house to look for Father.

DR. F. What else happens?

P. He looks at me and he doesn't say anything. I think he knows, but he doesn't do anything or say anything.

DR. F. How do you feel about that?

P. [Pause.] I feel . . . like . . . there's nothing he can do.

DR. F. And now I'd like you to move forward in time to the next important event, something that you need to know. One . . . two . . . three.

132

P. The man comes back. He's giving Father some money—[Short laugh.]—for me.

DR. F. How do you know that?

P. Because I'm . . . he's picking me up, putting me on his horse and we're leaving.

DR. F. How do you feel?

P. Afraid. [A tear runs down her cheek.]

DR. F. What do you think is happening?

P. He's taking me away.

DR. F. When do you think you'll be coming back?

P. I don't.

DR. F. Is he saying anything to you?

P. No.

DR. F. Move forward in time to the time you arrive at his place. What are you experiencing?

P. He has . . . a nice house, much better than ours. It's clean. He has food and, mmm, I'm so hungry.

DR. F. When you get to the house, what does he do?

P. He—he lets me eat.

DR. F. And what are you eating?

P. Beans, bread.

DR. F. Is anybody else in the house?

P. I think there is . . . I think there is a young girl. She's older than me.

DR. F. And then what happens?

P. He . . . tells me I'm there to work . . . that I . . . must . . . feed the chickens and clean the house with—with this other girl.

DR. F. What are your feelings about the other girl?

P. I don't know her. She seems okay.

DR. F. All right, now just move forward to the next significant event at the count of three. One . . . two . . . three.

P. She's telling me what happens there at that place.

DR. F. What does she say?

P. She says that he uses his girls—but he feeds them too, so they don't go hungry . . . so she stays, so she won't starve.

DR. F. In what way does he use them?

P. He . . . he does with them what he did to me.

DR. F. Are there other girls there now, other than this one?

P. Hmmm . . . I think there's just the girl and me.

DR. F. And now, Becky, just move forward in time to the next significant event at the count of three. One . . . two . . . three.

P. I hear her yelling. She's—she is with him now. I don't know what she's yelling about. [Becoming increasingly frightened.]

DR. F. Where are they?

P. They're in his room.

DR. F. What do you think is happening?

P. I think's happening—I—I think that he's . . . he's doing to her what he did to me.

DR. F. Looking at her and touching her?

P. Um-hmm.

DR. F. How do you feel as you hear her yelling?

P. I'm . . . I'm really afraid to leave, too.

DR. F. Why is that?

P. I don't want to be hungry.

DR. F. All right, now just move forward in time to the next significant event at the count of three. One . . . two . . . three.

P. I'm running away. I'm running through the desert . . . I don't have shoes, I can feel the cactus on my feet. [Terror in her voice.]

DR. F. When is it that you're running away? Is it the same day that you arrived?

P. No later.

DR. F. How long had you been with that man?

P. Not very long. Two days or . . . I stole some food. I'm running . . . I . . .

DR. F. What time of day is it?

P. Hot—the hot, hot time.

DR. F. Why are you running away, Becky?

P. I don't—I don't want to feel like I felt before with—I don't want him to do that to me.

DR. F. Did he do anything to you while you were at his home? It's okay to tell me.

P. He . . . he looked at me . . . he . . . he touched me and used his . . . his finger.

134

DR. F. How did you feel when he did that?

P. Uh . . . I felt afraid . . . I just wanted to get away.

DR. F. Okay, now I'd like you to go forward in time to the next significant event at the count of three. One . . . two . . . three.

P. I feel very tired, hot.

DR. F. Where are you?

P. I don't know.

DR. F. Are you still in the desert?

P. Um-hmm.

DR. F. Is it the same day that you started running away?

P. Yes.

DR. F. What's happening?

P. I feel . . . puffy all over . . . just puffy.

DR. F. Just look at yourself. Do you look any different?

P. I look . . . fat. I . . . I can't move. [Said with total bewilderment.]

DR. F. Can't move?

P. No, I just . . . I'm too fat to move. [Becoming upset.]

DR. F. What are you doing?

P. I'm lying.

DR. F. What do you think caused you to be like this?

P. Something bit me.

DR. F. When was that?

P. Oh . . . a while ago, when I was running.

DR. F. Did you see it?

P. I think it was a . . . a snake bit me. I tried to move, but . . .

DR. F. What else are you aware of, Becky?

P. The sun, very hot . . . feeling even weaker than when I was hungry . . . I'm so puffy. I feel like I'm gonna explode. [Voice sounds weaker.]

DR. F. Do you have any pain?

P. Just the tightness of my skin.

DR. F. Just go up to the next significant event at the count of three. One . . . two . . . three.

P. I hear someone coming, but I'm feeling so weak . . .

DR. F. What are you doing, Becky?

P. Just . . . just lying there. There's nothing I can do, I can't move.

DR. F. How do you feel?

P. I feel . . . I don't feel anything.

DR. F. Do you still feel puffy?

P. Very.

DR. F. Now just see what happens. Who's that coming?

P. I think it's . . . it's the girl.

DR. F. Is she walking?

P. No, she's riding.

DR. F. On a horse?

P. Um-hmm.

DR. F. Does she see you?

P. Yes.

DR. F. What does she do?

P. She picks me up.

DR. F. And now what?

P. We're riding back to the place. I . . . I don't wanna go, but I have no strength.

DR. F. Are you sitting up?

P. She's—she's holding me.

DR. F. Now just move forward in time at the count of three to the next significant event. One . . . two . . . three.

P. I don't feel puffy anymore.

DR. F. What's happened? Is anyone taking care of you?

P. The girl.

DR. F. What did she do?

P. She . . . she gave me something to drink, made the puffiness go away.

DR. F. Was it some kind of medicine?

P. Something she got in the desert.

DR. F. Some herbs, or some vegetation?

P. Um-hmm.

DR. F. How long has it been since you've been back in the house?

P. I don't know.

DR. F. Have you seen the man?

P. He's been away.

DR. F. Now go forward to the next significant event at the count of three. One . . . two . . . three.

P. [Long silence.]

DR. F. What are you aware of?

P. Hmmm . . . something smells sweet . . . hmm, I'm lying with my . . . with my arms—my arms are crossed.

DR. F. Where are they?

P. They're crossed over my—my chest. I'm . . . lying in a box. The girl has brought flowers.

DR. F. What are you doing in the box?

P. I'm . . . I'm no longer in . . . in my body.

DR. F. Where are you?

P. I'm . . . somewhere, but I can see I'm lying there. It's me.

DR. F. Are you looking at yourself?

P. Yes.

DR. F. And you're smelling something sweet?

P. Um-hmm.

DR. F. Who is there, besides the girl?

P. The girl is there.

DR. F. Is there anybody else there?

P. No.

DR. F. Where is the box?

P. It's . . . it's in the desert.

DR. F. Is it covered?

P. No, she's looking at me.

DR. F. She's there alone?

P. Yes.

DR. F. And now what is she doing?

P. She's walking away.

DR. F. And now what are you doing?

P. I'm . . . just . . . I'm lying in the box.

DR. F. Do you feel like you're back in your body again?

P. No.

DR. F. Where are you?

P. I'm floating.

DR. F. Are you alone?

P. I don't feel alone. [Voice sounds stronger now.] I don't feel anything. I don't feel the heat.

DR. F. You don't feel puffy?

P. No.

DR. F. What are your emotions right now?

P. Hmmm, I'm satisfied. I . . . I don't . . . I'm . . . I feel . . . [Long silence.] I don't, I don't feel . . . joy . . . it's peace, I don't—I'm not afraid . . . hmm . . . I'm suspended.

DR. F. And as you look back on the life as Becky, can you tell me when she lived?

P. Was the time of drought . . . Eighteen forty-nine?

DR. F. Looking back on Becky, did anything happen to her sexually other than the man touching her?

P. Yes. She wouldn't say.

DR. F. Will you say? It's all right for you to tell me, I'm here to help you.

P. Oh, he tried to put his . . . his penis in her, but it wouldn't work.

DR. F. Why was that?

P. She was too small.

DR. F. Is that when she decided to run away?

P. Yes.

After coming out of the trance, Patricia looked very sad. She said, "Becky experienced the whole range of feelings: anger, humiliation, fear and some sexual feelings going on too in myself and that was confusing." She stared straight into my eyes and I could sense her deep pity for what she, as Becky, had gone through. Tears were in her eyes. She lapsed into a thoughtful silence. This time Mark was not involved in her past life experience. She sounded tired and puzzled as she wondered, "Do you think that is it? Are there any more lifetimes we need to go through?" I shrugged my shoulders. Only *her* inner mind knew the answer to that question.

Indeed her inner mind did answer my questions early in her next session. We still had one more lifetime to explore.

Under hypnosis, she easily slipped back through the years to an event that had to do with the problem that kept her from fully enjoying herself sexually.

DR. F. What are you experiencing?

P. There's lots of foliage . . . it's . . . it's very thick and green.

DR. F. You're outside?

P. Um-hmm.

DR. F. What else are you aware of?

P. I'm standing on a plain looking into the . . . looking across the river.

DR. F. And what are you wearing?

P. Umm . . . it's—it's animal . . . fur. It's . . . it's called . . . umm . . . tupa.

DR. F. Tupa?

P. Um-hmm. It's what—it's what the women wear.

DR. F. Tell me more about yourself. What do you look like?

P. I don't—I don't see myself.

DR. F. What are you doing there besides just looking across the river?

P. Fishing.

DR. F. Tell me more.

P. I'm fishing for . . . for . . . our night feed.

DR. F. What do you use to catch the fish with?

P. Sharp stick. Have to . . . have to be fast—except for the big fish and they're slow. They're easy to get, but they don't taste as good.

DR. F. How often do you fish?

P. Every day. I have to . . . I have to be watchful. I'm on the other side of the river and some—something might get me. I have to—I have to watch.

DR. F. What are you afraid might get you?

P. The big cats or . . . another tribe.

DR. F. What is the name of your people?

P. Shulu.

DR. F. Shulu? What country are you in?

P. [Silence.]

DR. F. Do you know?

P. No.

DR. F. Tell me about yourself. Do you have children? Are you married?

P. I have . . . I have a man. I have no . . . no babies yet.

139

DR. F. How do you feel about your man?

P. He makes me . . . do the work. [Frowning.]

DR. F. Is that the custom of your people or does he make you work more than the other women?

P. More. He mostly just sits and makes spears. He doesn't want to go out with the others for the hunt. The other tribespeople . . . they laugh—at us because he—he won't go. He . . . I guess he's afraid. [Her voice full of contempt.]

DR. F. Do people get hurt on these hunts?

P. Yes.

DR. F. What about other tribes? Do you have problems with them?

P. Yes.

DR. F. Can you tell me more about that?

P. We . . . we're strong, but sometimes the other tribes will challenge us for our spot. We—we've won, but we may not always.

DR. F. When they challenge you, do they come into your village?

P. Yes. At night, usually.

DR. F. What do they do?

P. They try to . . . to kill our men and . . . but they haven't. I don't know what else they do. I don't . . . don't like that.

DR. F. What else do you do besides fish? Do you have any other duties or things that you like to do?

P. I pick fruit.

DR. F. What kind of fruit?

P. Off . . . off the bushes. It's—it's berries.

DR. F. Now, you said that you're on the other side of the river and you have to be watchful. Are you there alone?

P. Yes.

DR. F. Why did you go to the other side of the river?

P. Because that's where . . . that's where I can fish from.

DR. F. How do you get across the river?

P. We've made—we've put boards . . . trees . . . we can—we can walk across without going into the water.

DR. F. Are you still up on that plain looking across the river?

P. Um-hmm.

DR. F. All right. And now I'd like you to move forward in time to the next significant event at the count of five. One . . . two . . . three . . . four . . . five.

P. I'm back at our hut. He's still sitting there. We don't speak. He knows . . . I feel ashamed of him. He doesn't care. [Biting her lip.]

DR. F. How long have you been together?

P. Hmmm.

DR. F. It doesn't matter if you don't know. It will come to you later perhaps. Just go on and see what else happens as you are home.

P. Have to . . . clean fish. Have to . . . I . . . have to clean them . . . bite fishes' heads off.

DR. F. You bite it off with your teeth?

P. Yes.

DR. F. How do you feel about that?

P. It's just something that has to be done, then can put a sharp stick inside and rip open its belly. Then can clean it out and boil it.

DR. F. And now move forward in time to the next significant event at the count of five. One . . . two . . . just concentrating on your breathing and letting that memory fade as the new one begins to come in . . . three . . . four . . . five.

P. Hmm . . . it's nighttime. It's the time I hate most. Now is when he gets up . . . [Resignation and anger in her voice.]

DR. F. What do you mean "gets up"?

P. He . . . comes to bed . . . and he wants to . . . to try for . . . ah . . . for babies. I want babies, but . . . I don't . . . like to be with him.

DR. F. You don't like to be with him?

P. No. He's not a warrior.

DR. F. You feel ashamed to be with him?

P. Um-hmm. If we have sons, I hope they're . . . not weak like he is.

DR.F. So you don't want to be with him in that way?

P. No, I don't like him . . . but he is my man. If I want babies . . . we have to do this . . . so we do.

DR. F. How is it for you?

P. It's nothing.

DR. F. How often does this happen?

P. Each night . . . until . . . until I'm with a baby and then not until after it's . . . it's born. I can . . . can do that.

DR. F. You can do that?

P. Um-hmm.

DR. F. Is that because you want to have babies?

P. Yes.

DR. F. Do you get any pleasure out of it?

P. No! [With a snort.]

DR. F. What about the other women in your tribe? Do they talk about how they feel doing it?

P. Some of them are pleased. Some have . . . have good men and they tell me of things I can't believe.

DR. F. Like what?

P. That it . . . brings them pleasure, feelings of . . . like—like the sun, just pleasure. I . . . I don't know.

DR. F. And now I'd like your inner mind to take you to the next significant event at the count of five. One . . . two . . . three . . . four . . . five.

P. [Her face lights up with a smile.] I am . . . I am with child. Going to . . . to have a baby.

DR. F. How do you feel about that?

P. Ohh, good.

DR. F. And does your man come to you every night again?

P. No.

DR. F. Is that the custom of your people?

P. It is unless the woman still wants it . . . and I just don't.

DR. F. How does he react to your saying no?

P. He doesn't care. [Frowning again.] He . . . he's like a rock. He doesn't . . . he doesn't care . . . he has no—he has no sun—no inner sun—he is—he's . . . he's like—like a rock.

DR. F. And now I'd like you to move ahead five years

or so to a significant event at the count of five. One
. . . two . . . three . . . four . . . five.

P. There's my boy. [Said with much pride in voice.]
He's—he's brought much happiness to me. I'm not
. . . not completely ashamed anymore. [Voice softer now.] He will be—he'll be a good warrior. The
men—the other men already train him. He is—he's
already—he's killed a—a monkey, a big monkey and
he's—he's yet young. [Her motherly pride very apparent.]

DR. F. So you feel proud?

P. Oh, yes. He . . . he'll be very, very good.

DR. F. What is your son's name?

P. Shittu.

DR. F. What is your name?

P. Zawn.

DR. F. Do you know the country you live in, the name
of the place where you live?

P. I have . . . I heard some boat—boaters speaking.
They said it was . . . the Dark Place . . . big . . .
I don't know.

DR. F. Okay, now I'd like you to move ahead to the last
day of your life at the count of five, staying calm and
relaxed. One . . . two . . . three . . . four . . .
five.

P. Hmm . . . my son's there looking at me. He's
standing over me. [Her voice sounds weaker.] I feel
a great pride in him. I don't mind leaving.

DR. F. What is his expression?

P. Hmm. . . grief.

DR. F. Your man, is he there too?

P. Hmmm . . . no. He's—no, he isn't.

ff1DR. F. Where is he?

P. He's . . . he's dead.

DR. F. Do you have other children?

P. No.

DR. F. Are you an old woman?

P. Yes.

DR. F. How do you know that you're leaving?

P. Ohh . . . I can feel the . . . I've been told I'm

very sick and that I will be leaving soon—and I feel very weak.

DR. F. In what way are you sick?

P. I'm just . . . old.

DR. F. What do you feel happens to you when you die, after you leave? What is your belief?

P. My inner sun . . . goes out of my old body and I mingle with the other—others that have left. It's—if your life was at peace, so will be your sun.

DR. F. Do you feel that your life has been at peace?

P. Yes, I had my boy. [Smiling.] He's my pride.

DR. F. Do you feel that your sun comes back into another body at another time?

P. I . . . don't . . . know.

DR. F. And now I'd like you to go to the very moment of your death and tell me what's happening and what you do, and what your son does.

P. He's putting ashes on my body and chanting.

DR. F. Is anyone else there with you?

P. There are some people.

DR. F. Have you left yet? Has your inner sun left yet?

P. Hmm . . . no.

DR. F. And what are you experiencing?

P. I feel like I am not in my body. I'm not . . . where I should be.

DR. F. Tell me more.

P. I feel in-between . . . I'm no longer a part of that existence. I'm not part of the other existence. I am . . . I'm not either.

DR. F. Are you alone?

P. I feel alone.[A peaceful look on her face.]

DR. F. As you look back on your life, do you have any knowledge of where it is that this lifetime took place and the time period?

P. It was in Africa . . . I can't say when.

DR. F. Does it seem like a recent time or a long time ago?

P. It seems recent. I feel close.

DR. F. Can you describe what you looked like when you were a young person, what the color of your skin and

144

what your hair looked like, your stature and so forth.

P. I was very black, just . . . darker than most. My hair was straight, it was . . . straight, coarse hair.

DR. F. How long did you wear it? In what style?

P. I wore it to my shoulders. I took a stick and creased—got the skin line and combed my hair straight down.

DR. F. Did you wear any ornaments on your body?

P. They . . . were shells of nuts and teeth and claws.

DR. F. Were these around your neck?

P. Yes.

DR. F. Did you have any other ornaments or did you do anything else to your body to decorate it?

P. I had . . . a hole in my ear and I had a—the monkey's bone through my ear to show my pride for my son when he was small.

DR. F. Was that from his first monkey?

P. Yes.

I asked Patricia to return to the present and herself—and then brought her out of trance. She said, "This regression was the most vivid of all and it felt very recent to me." I asked her, "Was your man someone you know in this life?" She said, "Yes—I had the feeling all along it was Mark."

As she got up to leave, she turned and commented, "I hope we will be finished with our work soon." She added, smiling, "What I just experienced explains a lot to me. I've still been falling asleep often during the week—more than I would like. I wonder whether this regression will improve things with Mark?"

As she closed the door behind her, I sat down and mentally got in touch again with all the facets of Patricia I had met in just a few months: haughty Alena, the Kauaian princess; poor Kim who hated herself so much she dashed herself to death; Tia, fat and scared of being hurt; lonely Meteus who was so brutally raped; little Becky who was also abused; and now Zawn whose only joy was her son. What a fascinating array of past personalities—each so completely different from the others

145

and each having contributed so substantially to Patricia's remarkable initial problem. With the tremendous progress she had made so far, there couldn't be any more—or many more. Or could there?

During the next session we determined under hypnosis that there were no more lifetimes contributing to Patricia's sexual problems! Indeed, there was hardly a problem left at this point. Her account of their love-making was glowing. Each week I had expected her to come in with the good news that she had reached a climax. Because she hadn't, and from her description of their love-making, I felt they only needed to develop a slightly different pattern in their sexual technique. I asked them to come in together.

The following week we discussed the progress they had made. Mark pointed out that they now had a warm, harmonious and close relationship. They really enjoyed doing many things together. The fighting was almost totally a thing of the past. It was hard now for him to tell when Patricia's menstrual periods were about to start—and that was a real miracle, he exclaimed. Patricia added that lately when they had been at parties she didn't feel the least shred of jealousy and even found herself at ease with the other women there.

They had both acquired absorbing hobbies through these months. And Patricia even made a decision to give up working and go back to college. I enjoyed hearing them being so supportive of each other—and describing the other's skills and natural talents. Their love for each other was shining in their faces.

I gave them a few pointers on sexual techniques and *knew* that it would be just a matter of a few weeks before I said goodbye to Patricia and Mark as patients.

Within three weeks, they came in together—unexpectedly—for Patricia's appointment. With big smiles on their faces they presented me with another beautiful bouquet of flowers. I felt a tremendous happiness for both of these lovely warm people who had grown to be friends. I was aware within myself of a deep, good feeling, the feeling of having shared many rich experiences and of our having grown so close. As they were leaving, with tears in their eyes, I felt sad and happy at the same time.

❦

CHAPTER SEVEN

"Fear, Fear, and a . . . Terror!"

"Even my wife doesn't know. I use all kinds of excuses, except the real one," Mike revealed with guilt written all over his face. His problem? An inexplicable fear of heights. He described the anxiety he felt in high places as escalating to terror at times. Sitting before me was a tall, slim, tanned, stylishly bearded attorney in his mid-forties. He nervously tapped his fingers on the arm of the chair and avoided looking directly at me as he continued to explain why he was seeking help. He painted a portrait of himself as a master of evasion, one who avoided social and business appointments that required driving over bridges or into mountainous areas. His business losses were incalculable because of these restrictions. Still, he managed to become financially successful. He shook his head gloomily as he talked of what he would be doing if only he had the freedom to get in his car and go anywhere. Or get into a plane, which was totally out of the question for him. He regretted having to deny his wife, and himself, the pleasure of visiting relatives and touring Europe. Mike was proud. This fear didn't fit into his self-image, so he covered it up from everyone—family, friends and business acquaintances. Over the years he had unburdened himself to a host of therapists—one an orthodox Freudian analyst in New York City, another who conducts weekend marathon encounter groups, and a third who specializes in phobias, a practitioner well-known for his special "confront-and-conquer" approach. Despite the efforts of all involved in his treatment, his phobia persisted unabated.

Mike was psychologically sophisticated. He had been

in treatment for so many years that he "knew" the reasons for his fear. He had concluded that he had a tremendous fear of dying, paradoxically coupled with a strong drive to destroy himself. He was convinced his problem was really a literal terror of losing control and harming himself or others. Yet this didn't fit in with the rest of his life. He had a successful marriage, good relationships with his children and had done remarkably well in his career. He was well-liked and had many close friends. He also enjoyed sports and was deeply interested in music. He admitted to a great passion for the opera. As he put it, "I have a zest for living!"

Mike was sitting in my office because he had caught the tail-end of a radio program, just enough to hear about my work in past lives. His curiosity was aroused—and he was desperate. He was afraid he could not be hypnotized. Yes, he had tried that, too! But it amounted to just one appointment in a hypnosis clinic.

Our first session was scheduled for two hours, as he had come for a past-life regression. After interviewing him, I taught him self-hypnosis and then led him back into the distant past. He slipped into a deep trance and was able easily to see scenes in fine detail. But what we were getting were kaleidoscopic vignettes—flashes of scenes that seemed to emanate from many different lifetimes. One "series" stood out from the other images. He described seeing a roof of a very large Gothic structure. The next scene contained a casket. These were followed by a few other glimpses of death scenes. Our time was up and we still had a great deal of work to do. We decided to set up a standing appointment to meet once a week.

During the weeks that followed, Mike's inner mind took us through a maze. We looked at many events from the past—some in this lifetime and others in former lives. He seemed to be dealing with other problems and skirting the events that led to his crippling phobia.

One day he came in beaming. I had given him a posthypnotic suggestion the week before that his subconscious mind would prepare him to look at the material he needed to understand, and that he would gain insight

149

through dreams or as flashes during the day. He reported a very powerful—and frightening—fragment of a dream which had a tremendously releasing effect on him. He saw a man's body with the head impaled on a wooden structure. The face was distorted with agony. The body and everything nearby was covered with blood. He saw it all in vivid "technicolor." He looked at the scene quickly twice just to make sure the man was dead. That's all he could stand. He repeated many times while recalling and discussing the dream that he had "never seen it before." Although the dream was just a flash, "it was unbelievably horrible." But in the time that followed he felt a great surge of self-confidence, a sureness that lasted for days. He was excited about his change, seeing it as a first major step toward his goal of freedom.

He settled back in the chair, eager to be hypnotized. When he was in a deep trance, I asked his inner mind to take him back to the lifetime that he had dreamed of just a few days before. His eyes moved under their closed lids. He turned his head from side to side as though he were looking around at something. Hesitantly, and in a soft, uncertain voice he began to describe what he was seeing:

M. Ahh . . . people . . . I . . . I see what I think is myself.

DR. F. Please describe that person.

M. Balding.

DR. F. Can you tell me more about him?

M. Dark hair . . . and ah . . . beard . . . smiling.

DR. F. What is he doing?

M. It looks as though he's talking to several people on a—on a sidewalk or stonewalk. I'm not sure whether it's a sidewalk or street.

DR. F. How is he dressed?

M. He's got a bag over his arm—over his shoulder—slung over . . . carrying tools of some kind.

DR. F. He's carrying some kind of tools?

M. Yeah, looks like it . . . work clothes, smock or

something. Seems to be addressing somebody on the street.

DR. F. What is the setting?

M. Oh, it's pleasant. Sky is blue . . . and a lot of tile roofs. [Mumbling.]

DR. F. What kind of roofs?

M. They're tile . . . red and some pink . . . orange tile.

DR. F. What color are the buildings?

M. Look like . . . plaster. Stucco or plaster.

DR. F. You will become aware of what they're talking about at the count of three. One . . . two . . . three.

M. Well, the first thing—that I hear—the words "broken tile."

DR. F. "Broken tile"?

M. Well, those words just come to me. I assume that that was what the discussion was . . . and the tools in the bag for and a . . . I don't know, I was just out, in front of these . . . buildings . . . and one seemed rather high—two stories, you know.

DR. F. What kind of building was that?

M. I can't see the . . . can't make it out.

DR. F. It will become clearer and clearer and clearer. One . . . two . . . three . . . four . . . five.

M. Looks like a big church . . . huge old church.

DR. F. What kind of church did you say? [Remembering the dream, I wondered if we were at last solving the riddle.]

M. Huge . . . Gothic-type church—at least it seems so.

DR. F. Can you tell me some more about your surroundings and what you're aware of?

M. There are some people there—old ladies. I'm just sort of walking up to the altar . . . seems I'm looking for something.

DR. F. Now you will become aware of what you're looking for at the count of three. One . . . two . . . three.

M. [Big sigh.] I'm looking for a priest—or somebody there—or brother or somebody that . . .

151

DR. F. Why are you looking for a priest?

M. I don't know what it's in conjunction with at all.

DR. F. Do you still have your bag of tools with you?

M. Yes.

DR. F. At the count of three you will know why you're looking for a priest. Just remain calm and relaxed. One . . . two . . . three. Whatever comes to mind.

M. [Breathing hard.] Well, I see him raise his hand or . . . to the roof.

DR. F. To the roof?

M. I'm not sure who that is, whether it's a priest or . . .

DR. F. You see someone raising his hand to the roof?

M. Yes, it's kind of blocking out . . . pointing back towards—that side, that right side.

DR. F. And what is he saying? At the count of three, just get in touch with the gist of what he's saying. One . . . two . . . three.

M. I don't . . . the only thing, I guess . . . I see myself in another scene, crawling out a hole—in the side of the roof . . . it's a window, round, or octagon-shaped window . . . and there's a—ladder up to that . . . and I'm out of the roof. Seems to be—quite high . . . tile, again. Seems to be somebody else up there. This is a . . . a . . . one of those wings . . . old churches were designed—in the form of crosses . . . you had your long entry way going up to the middle and then you had the two side walls . . . two side . . . and I'd apparently crawled through one on the side on the left to get around up to the right for what reason, I don't know.

DR. F. You say there's somebody else up there?

M. [Wiping his hands on his pants.] Um-hmm. I don't know why my hands should be perspiring.

DR. F. Just stay calm and relaxed. Now what do you see happening? What are you doing now?

M. Just working on the tile . . . with a . . . out of my bag.

DR. F. Tell me how you're working on it. What kinds of tools are you using? What do you do to it?

M. They are iron tools. Ah . . . metal tools with, kind

152

of like the crowbar to raise tiles up and replace rotted timbers and rotten substances where water has leaked in and caulk and a little hammer and little . . . kind of a . . . hammer on one side and a cutting or chipping tool on the other.

DR. F. Is this your specialty, to take care of roofs—broken tiles?

M. I don't know. Somebody seems to be directing . . . and somebody else seems to be talking to me, but I don't know . . . seems to be in conjunction with the work, but I don't know what he's saying.

DR. F. I'm going to count from one to three and then you will know. One . . . two . . . three. And whatever comes to mind.

M. When I get finished on that side, go to the right side.

DR. F. Why is that? Is there something on the other side?

M. Yes. Because I'm not working on that side, I'm working on the . . . the left side—looking to the front.

DR. F. And how do you feel as you're up there working?

M. Well, it's sort of—high and stratified and kind of . . . I don't . . . I had a feeling when I first came out that it . . . you know, it was high, to watch my step. [His face breaks out in beads of sweat.]

DR. F. What do you have on your feet?

M. They seem to be tied on to me. It's some kind of a thing to keep my feet from slipping, but I—can't make out what it is.

DR. F. Is it some kind of a sandal that is tied on to your leg?

M. Yeah, soft leather, to . . . you'll need to walk up there—and a . . .without falling . . . feels like—it's getting a little wet.

DR. F. Why is it getting wet?

M. Must be raining.

DR. F. Just get in touch with what's happening. What are you experiencing?

M. [Breathing fast now.] Well, when I first came up there, it . . . it's colors that I don't see here often . . . it's a . . . different, it looks like the southern

part of . . . Europe . . . with those kind of hills—
and this church seems to be on a hill. There are other
hills—and places where there are houses and what-
have-you in stucco and . . . fog, blue fog and mist
and . . .

DR. F. And how long have you been working on the
roof before it starts to rain?

M. I don't know. I can't . . . it just does . . . and
what time elapsed I don't know. I was just working
on this side and on the gutters, I see the green copper
gutters . . .

DR. F. And tell me more. What are you experiencing?

M. Oh, I was just looking at the gutters and around—
the cornices of the church—and feeling a little anxiety.

DR. F. Why is that?

M. Looking down. Looking down—as it's quite high.

DR. F. Is it raining hard?

M. No . . . no. Just that I'm aware that . . . whether
it's from rain or mist or what, but they are wet. The
tiles are wet. And I'm being particularly cautious.
But it's my work . . . and I seem to know . . . my
way around.

DR. F. Now what are you doing?

M. I'm getting up and crossing over to the other side,
and I'm making a cursory inspection of . . . of, ah
. . . seems that this priest is wearing a skull cap and
a robe.

DR. F. Is the priest up on the roof, too?

M. Yeah . . . and he's the one directing me.

DR. F. Now what are you aware of?

M. I'm just looking down at the . . . apparently trying
to find the area. He's standing up at the ridge of the
roof or slightly to the left side, looking down at me.
And I'm aware of the heights. [Becoming visibly upset.]

DR. F. How are you feeling now? I notice you're clench-
ing your fists, rubbing your hands.

M. Ah, just a little . . . moist . . . whether it's from
holding . . .

DR. F. Now what are you aware of?

154

M. I'm aware of losing some tools—rolling down the side and . . . kind of lying flat . . . I don't know whether I'm reaching for them or what.

DR. F. Just get in touch with what happens. Just tell me what comes next. What are you aware of?

M. Well, somehow there's some loose tiles and that enters into this. Where the hell it goes, I . . . I don't know, it just seems to be that the part . . . the loss of tools is something, falling down and reaching them . . . giving away and . . . my hanging, dangling on the gutter and the tiles and . . . that's a . . . and it seems that it's three stories high . . . it's just high!

DR. F. Where are you now?

M. I . . . I'm hanging on that damn, ah . . .

DR. F. On what?

M. I'm hanging on that . . . gutter and grabbing some of these tiles that are loose and broken—but they're not much help and they're falling.

DR. F. Where is your body?

M. I'm off the side, hanging . . . just . . . I'd say, arm on the gutter or . . . one hand in the gutter and the other arm on the top of the . . . but I stay right there. I don't seem to . . . fall. [Face bathed in sweat.]

DR. F. Where is the priest? Is he there?

M. No . . . gone.

DR. F. What are you experiencing? Get in touch with your feelings.

M. [Long pause.]

DR. F. What are you aware of? What thoughts go through your mind?

M. Well, I . . . I don't . . . I . . . I . . . I . . . I have anxiety, but I don't have the terror of falling. I don't have the . . . I don't see this . . . I kind of stop there. I don't . . . I'm aware of the buildings.

DR. F. What buildings are you aware of?

M. The building I'm on . . . the church and . . . where I am, in what position and where, what a . . . don't . . . go beyond falling . . . there.

DR. F. You're still dangling, you're hanging onto the

155

gutter and your body is dangling and your one arm is grasping for tiles above?

M. [Nods head yes.]

DR. F. I'm going to ask you to concentrate on your breathing. I'm going to count from one to three and you'll become much more relaxed and calm and your inner mind will let you proceed step by step so that you can see what happens to yourself. One . . . just becoming very relaxed as you experience what's happening . . . two . . . three. What are you aware of?

M. There are some people trying to help . . . standing on the other side letting down something—a rope or something.

DR. F. Now what? Are they saying anything to you?

M. I am, well . . . partially, holding on to that rope . . . and I am grabbing at the gutter, the tiles . . . and I'm swinging back and forth.

DR. F. What are you feeling?

M. I feel the swaying and the . . . the precarious position I'm in. [Squirming.]

DR. F. What emotions are you experiencing?

M. Fear, fear, and a . . . terror! I mean, I'm just trying to hang on the best I can . . . [Covering his face with his hands.] One of them lets go and I lost . . .

DR. F. One of the people lets go?

M. Yes.

DR. F. And then what happens?

M. My full weight went on the gutter and it broke.

DR. F. Go on. Now what's happening? The gutter broke?

M. Yes.

DR. F. Tell me what you're experiencing.

M. That whole thing is . . . the whole gutter is coming down—with some tile pieces and fragments.

DR. F. What are you aware of?

M. Well, I just see myself falling. At first it was me, then I . . . pulled away and saw somebody falling.

DR. F. Can you see his face, can you see his body as he falls?

M. Backwards . . . face up.

DR. F. Falling with his back to the ground?

M. Right.

DR. F. Head first?

M. No, his body's . . . back and forward first . . . is back and forward first and his hands held in the air where he was holding onto the . . . and straight out, spread out. [Demonstrating, his arms stretched out.]

DR. F. What is he doing as he's falling?

M. Just . . .

DR. F. Do you hear anything?

M. Just faintly. Just faintly.

DR. F. You will hear.

M. Well, kind of a yell . . . I hear a yell—I don't know if it's from him or not. Ah . . .

DR. F. What are you experiencing now?

M. Well, I'm either . . . "Oh, my God!" . . . that's . . .

DR. F. He's saying, "Oh, my God!"?

M. Yeah.

DR. F. And now what's going on?

M. That's all I can seem to . . . it's rather dark down there where he's falling . . . falling. I thought it was between two buildings, but it . . . maybe it's a . . . maybe it's a wall . . . wall . . . which makes it dark down there. But I can't see the body . . . down there.

DR. F. Just relax. Now I'm going to count from one to three and you will see the body. One . . . two . . . three. What do you see?

M. I see his impaled face. Well, I see a look of agony, I just . . . of death in its . . . complete form. He is on this . . . wood . . . scaffolding . . . it's gone almost through him, I mean, I just . . . it was . . . the horrible part about it . . . it looked like it had been, you know . . . he'd just been *forced*, you know . . . fell upon this or . . . I don't know, I don't know. I mean this is a . . . [Breathing rapidly.] I can look back up.

DR. F. What comes to mind? What are you experiencing now?

M. I'm just observing the building. I want to take the whole building in . . . I see the broken drain. I see all the . . . way up high above me and the sky. It's kind of turned white now.

DR. F. Where are you now?

M. Below, looking up.

DR. F. Are you on the ground?

M. On the ground, lying flat.

DR. F. And now what are you aware of? What are your thoughts as you're lying there?

M. I don't seem to grasp that. I just see . . . people around and . . . somebody trying to help me . . . somebody raising my head.

DR. F. And now what happens?

M. Well, it seems that it gets darker and darker . . . sort of like blotting out the sun . . . I seem to be . . . not to be able to see . . . but a feeling of what's going on . . . around me . . . the people are staring and frightened and . . . and I see essentially the same—party I saw before.

DR. F. Tell me again. Who was he?

M. In that dream . . . not in the same position, but lying—flat . . .

DR. F. The same face?

M. Pretty close . . . it's just not as vivid . . . just a . . . that was just a . . . blinding flash. That thing was . . . and on and off. . . this is not that. This is . . . this is the party I saw standing out front of it I guess, it was the church, the buildings. Sort of friendly, blue eyes.

As he came out of the trance, Mike smiled weakly at me. He was obviously emotionally exhausted by the trauma he had just relived. He wiped the sweat from his face with his hands, ran his fingers through his hair and got up abruptly. He wanted to escape the scene of so much psychic pain. We had run overtime, so he left after confirming his next week's appointment.

After he left, I sank back into my chair. This regression had been draining for me, too. I reviewed it in my mind, remembering his reactions, especially the anxiety he had so obviously experienced. I recalled his switching from himself as participant to an observer-reporter. He tried to spare himself panic and pain by avoiding facing the situation time after time. This had made it very difficult for him to approach the issue of the fall. I felt that we had pinpointed the event responsible for his fear of heights, but I sensed that he needed really to experience the feeling itself in order to get the relief he sought—and needed. I felt empathy for him, and sorry for him. It would be rough going through that again!

CHAPTER EIGHT

"Just Listening . . . Watching"

When Joe came for help he was desperate. He *had* to solve his problem, severe insomnia. Most nights he could not get to sleep until dawn, unless he took four sleeping pills—all at the same time. He always paid the price, sleeping twelve hours and being hung over for many more. Night after night he would lie awake resisting the pills. Without fail, his head would swim in a stream of inconsequential thoughts. As is so often the case with symptoms, his insomnia was causing other problems. He found it impossible to concentrate. And he needed concentration because he was preparing for a real estate exam. It was imperative that he memorize page after page of facts and laws. Sleep eluding him, he worried about passing the exam—which made it harder for him to sleep at night. Around and around it went.

Joe was a trim man in his mid-thirties. He did not carry an extra pound on his medium-sized frame. He dressed impeccably in flamboyant shirts, well-fitting slacks and polished cowboy boots. There was an air about him that instantly said, "I am an individualist."

Joe had seen me originally for his three-pack-a-day smoking habit. But this time he came in response to a lecture I gave at a local college. When I traced the causes of several cases of sleep disorders back to former lives, his interest was piqued. He called for an appointment the very next day.

Under hypnosis, Joe's subconscious mind indicated, through finger signals, that his problem was traceable to two events from a past lifetime. I gave suggestions to his inner mind to prepare him at a subconscious level to look at this former life next time. As he was leaving, he paused at the door. "The idea of a previous existence intrigues me," he laughed. "I wonder who I was before."

He returned the next week. Within five minutes I started the hypnotic induction—I wanted to be able to use as much time as possible on his past-life regression. I rechecked his finger signals and found that his inner mind had prepared him. I proceeded with the regression, counting him back to "another place and time" and waited . . . and waited. Nothing came. He was experiencing "nothing." I was puzzled. I had a hunch he was resisting and probably needed more preparation. I gave him further hypnotic suggestions again to prepare for a past life regression during the week interval and brought him out of the trance. When we discussed what had happened, he revealed that he had seen a "general store and a street scene vividly"—even to the ruts in the dirt road and the worn wooden sidewalks. But he didn't say anything about it, because he thought he was "conjuring it up." When he started to leave, he said, "I understand now. Next time I'll trust my inner mind and report faithfully whatever comes up, whether it makes sense or not!"

As he walked into my office, he confessed that in the previous week as he was driving over for his appointment he felt very fearful—in fact, he was almost in a cold sweat. He assured me he was ready this time. I repeated the instructions to report everything. He slipped very quickly into a deep trance. After being regressed to a pleasant or neutral event during the childhood of the lifetime responsible for his sleep problem, he said:

J. I'm in the yard . . . just playing.
DR. F. Tell me more.
J. It's in front of the house. Just playing with a ball.
DR. F. How old are you?
J. Ten.
DR. F. And what is your name?
J. [Hesitates.] I can't . . .
DR. F. I'm going to count from one to three, and at the

161

count of three your name will come to you. One . . . two . . . three.

J. Dale.

DR. F. Dale, what's your last name?

J. Short.

DR. F. Tell me about yourself, Dale. Whom do you live with?

J. I live with my mother and father, my sister . . .

DR. F. Where?

J. Kentucky.

DR. F. What does your father do?

J. He's the marshal.

DR. F. How do you feel about him being the marshal?

J. I'm proud of him. [Smiling.]

DR. F. Now concentrate on your breathing, and your inner mind is moving you ahead to the next significant event at the count of five. One . . . two . . . three . . . four . . . five.

J. My father's dead.

DR. F. Did he just die?

J. He was killed.

DR. F. How was he killed, Dale?

J. Shot.

DR. F. Just found that out now?

J. Um-hmm.

DR. F. Who shot him, Dale?

J. Gunfighter.

DR. F. Tell me more about it.

J. I feel bad because of my mother and my little sister . . . I didn't think that ah . . . anybody could beat him.

DR. F. Really surprises you.

J. Um-hmm.

DR. F. Was he a very good shot?

J. Um-hmm. He was very fast. [His chin quivers, tears form.]

DR. F. I'm sorry to hear that . . . what will the family do?

J. My mother does dresses, makes dresses . . . I'm not gonna stay.

DR. F. Where are you going?

J. I'll go West.

DR. F. How old are you now, Dale?

J. Seventeen.

DR. F. Just let go of these feelings, these memories for the time being. Concentrate on your breathing as I count from one to five, becoming calm and relaxed. One . . . two . . . three . . . four . . . five. What are you experiencing now, Dale?

J. By a campfire. A lot of people.

DR. F. What's happening?

J. It's a wagon train.

DR. F. Is it nighttime?

J. Um-hmm.

DR. F. How old are you now?

J. Twenty.

DR. F. Have you been traveling long?

J. About five months.

DR. F. And where are you right now?

J. Just by the Rockies.

DR. F. What time of year is it?

J. It's in the springtime or summertime.

DR. F. Guess that's a good time to go over those Rockies.

J. It's warm.

DR. F. Tell me more about this evening.

J. I'm leaning against a wagon.

DR. F. How are you feeling?

J. Decided I'd join in with *these* people . . .

DR. F. You don't join in with those others?

J. No.

DR. F. Why is that?

J. They just know how to farm and . . . they're going out West to get land and . . . they're not prepared. [Sounding superior.]

DR. F. What do you mean by that?

J. They can't defend themselves.

DR. F. Do you feel that you are prepared?

J. Hm-hmm. Not in every way, but most . . . most ways.

DR. F. How would you defend yourself?

J. Just with my gun.

163

DR. F. You're a pretty good shot? How did you learn?

J. My father taught me.

DR. F. He was a very good shot, wasn't he?

J. Yeah.

DR. F. So you're sitting and you're kind of leaning against—is it *your* wagon you're leaning against?

J. Just have a horse.

DR. F. So you're leaning against one of the wagons . . . you've been traveling for five months now. When do you think you'll arrive where you're going?

J. Maybe couple months.

DR. F. Your destination?

J. California. No special place.

DR. F. What do you want to do when you get out there?

J. Maybe be a guard on a stagecoach or . . . bank or something.

DR. F. And now just let a little time pass and see what happens, if anything significant happens during this episode. I'm going to count from one to five and at the count of five, just let me know what you're experiencing now. One . . . two . . . three . . . four . . . five. What are you experiencing now, Dale?

J. Indians have ambushed us. [Breathing hard.]

DR. F. Tell me more about that.

J. We were going . . . approaching a pass and the Indians were . . . were hiding on the sides of the pass, and they started shooting at us.

DR. F. What were they shooting with?

J. Some rifles . . . bows and arrows.

DR. F. What has happened as a result of that?

J. We've had to leave . . . leave the wagons, because . . . we can't group the wagons . . . it's not a good defensive position.

DR. F. Everybody's left the wagons and what have they done?

J. We've run towards the trees.

DR. F. Where are you right now?

J. In among some trees.

DR. F. Tell me what you see.

J. There's Indians up there, too. On horses. [Looking up—body tenses.]

164

DR. F. Up where?

J. Among the trees.

DR. F. How do you feel?

J. I feel sorry for these people . . . half of them women . . . pulling them on their horses and riding off with them . . . these people can't hit anything they're shooting at. [Exasperated.]

DR. F. Just like sitting ducks then, aren't they? Anyone been killed yet?

J. Some Indians . . . I shot quite a few.

DR. F. You shot quite a few?

J. Um-hum. I shot one of the women . . . couldn't get a clear shot at the Indian.

DR. F. You accidentally hit the woman?

J. On purpose.

DR. F. That would be more merciful than letting her go?

J. She's better off. [Tears springing to his eyes.]

DR. F. Just staying calm and relaxed. You had a feeling that something like this would happen, didn't you?

J. Um-hum.

DR. F. Let all those memories go and move to the next significant event. One . . . two . . . three . . . four . . . five. What are you experiencing now, Dale?

J. I'm in the town . . . in the hills . . . mountains . . . it's a gold mining town.

DR. F. What are you doing right now?

J. Just walking down the sidewalk . . . miners, a lot of people—men.

DR. F. Where are you? What state are you in?

J. California.

DR. F. Have you been here long?

J. No, I just been here about a week or so.

DR. F. Looking back on that Indian raid, can you tell me what the outcome was?

J. [Long pause.] We held them off till that night . . . weren't very many left . . . told 'em to pass the word to try to just make it on their own . . . don't group up because the Indians would catch up and . . . they'd be better off alone. I left alone.

DR. F. You left at night?

J. Um-hmm.

DR. F. Were you tired by then?

J. No.

DR. F. How could you see the way?

J. Just . . . just by the moonlight and . . . maybe
the Indians would be tracking us the next morning . . . I don't think . . . [Deep sigh.] . . . the
others stand a chance.

DR. F. You think the others don't stand a chance but
you know much more what *you're* doing, don't you?

J. Um-hmm.

DR. F. Were you able to sleep that night?

J. No. The Indians were sneaking . . . around us . . .
got a couple with my knife that night.

DR. F. Your knife? That was pretty close fighting,
wasn't it?

J. Um-hmm.

DR. F. Were you all trying to get some sleep at that
point?

J. No!

DR. F. Wouldn't dare take a chance on that, would you?
About what time of night was that that happened?

J. It was all night.

DR. F. When was it that you left on your own?

J. About three hours before daylight.

DR. F. So all night long you were in kind of a camp with
the others or just in one area with the others?

J. In the woods.

DR. F. And you had to be really alert because those Indians could come up at any moment. They were all
around you?

J. We were . . . the others and I were fairly close to
each other.

DR. F. But you had to be alert, didn't you?

J. Um-hmm. Could hear someone scream every now
and then because . . . [Sighing deeply.] . . . Indian
had gotten them with a tomahawk or a knife.

DR. F. That must have been a terrible night for you.

J. I wasn't afraid. [Genuinely.]

DR. F. How did you spend your time that night before
you left?

J. Just listening . . . watching. There wasn't much you could see, though. Just the trees, no moonlight came in through there . . . good fighters.

DR. F. Who were they?

J. Crows.

DR. F. How could you tell that?

J. I just knew there were Crows in that area . . . Crows are the only hostile ones. Other tribes were peaceful.

DR. F. What you're saying is that you were there in the woods. You could hear screaming from time to time, but you weren't afraid. You were just being very alert.

J. Um-hmm.

DR. F. Because you knew that if you didn't pay attention, that could cost you your life, is that it?

J. Well, I was just thinking of protecting myself. There was no way I could help the group. [His voice sounding depressed.]

DR. F. And now, here you are in this mining town. And where are you right now?

J. I'm in the street.

DR. F. What are you doing, Dale?

J. Just going to the bars and saloons.

DR. F. What do you do there?

J. I'm not doing anything yet. I don't—I don't think I'll stay here. I'm just seeing what it's like.

DR. F. Now I'm going to ask you to move on to the next significant event at the count of five. Just letting go of these memories. One . . . two . . . three . . . four . . . five. What are you aware of?

J. I'm in Mexico.

DR. F. Tell me more about that.

J. I'm drinking and dancing with girls.

DR. F. Why are you in Mexico, Dale?

J. [Lowering his voice.] Just kind of . . . hiding.

DR. F. Hiding?

J. Um-hmm.

DR. F. Why are you hiding?

J. [Whispering.] I robbed a stagecoach . . . to get some money.

DR. F. Were you able to get some money that way?

J. Um-hmm.

DR. F. Can you tell me some more about it?

J. See, I'd run out of money and . . . mostly ranch work and . . . I don't like that kind of work. And I saw this stagecoach, so I robbed it . . . just ambushed 'em. Didn't kill anybody.

DR. F. Did you make that decision on the spur of the moment or had you planned it?

J. Kinda curious to see what it would be like.

DR. F. What was it like?

J. I didn't like it because I thought . . . one of the people would try to . . . shoot me and I'd have to kill 'em.

DR. F. But somehow you avoided that?

J. Um-hmm.

DR. F. How much money did you get?

J. Around fifteen hundred dollars—in gold!

DR. F. When was that?

J. Been maybe a month.

DR. F. And now you're down in Mexico and you're hiding out for a while?

J. I . . . I'll stay here for a while and then I'll go back up through Texas. I'd be wanted in California.

DR. F. Okay, now I'm going to count from one to five and on the count of five, I'd like you to move ahead to the next significant event. One . . . two . . . three . . . four . . . five. Where are you now, Dale?

J. I'm in a bar. They've got ah . . . gambling tables, dance girls . . . I keep fights from breaking out . . . I'm a guard there.

DR. F. What do you do?

J. I'm here to see that he doesn't get robbed.

DR. F. You mean so that the bar doesn't get robbed?

J. Um-hmm. There's a lot of money in there.

DR. F. Do you like your job?

J. Not really.

DR. F. How long have you been doing it?

J. Three months.

DR. F. Where are you now?

J. Texas.

DR. F. How old are you now, Dale?

J. I'm twenty-seven.

DR. F. Have you had any desire to get married?

J. No.

DR. F. Are you pretty much a loner?

J. Yes.

DR. F. Now, let go of these memories and move on to the next significant event at the count of five. One . . . two . . . three . . . four . . . five.

J. I'm on a stagecoach . . . as a guard . . . it's an easy job.

DR. F. Where's the stagecoach going?

J. To Wichita.

DR. F. Quite a distance, isn't it?

J. No.

DR. F. Do you like your work?

J. Not really. Better than ranchin' . . . being a cowhand.

DR. F. And now I'm going to ask you to let go of this memory and move ahead to the next significant event at the count of five. One . . . two . . . three . . . four . . . five. And whatever comes to mind.

J. I'm the sheriff.

DR. F. What state are you in now, Dale?

J. I'm still in Kansas.

DR. F. How do you like this job?

J. I like, I like it. [Smiling.]

DR. F. You like it lots better than being a guard?

J. Um-hmm.

DR. F. How long have you been sheriff?

J. Two years.

DR. F. So you've sort of settled down, haven't you, in this town?

J. Um-hmm. [Proudly.] People respect me here.

DR. F. What's the name of the town?

J. Pittsburg.

DR. F. Pittsburg? And what are you doing right now?

J. Just walkin' down the street . . . on the sidewalk . . . say "Hi" to the people. Not much to do during the daytime.

DR. F. Do you get busier at night?

169

J. Um-hmm.

DR. F. What kind of town is . . .

J. Stores . . . and the . . . bar, they're always getting drunk and shootin' each other. [Impatiently.]

DR. F. Have you married yet, Dale?

J. No.

DR. F. How old are you now?

J. Twenty-nine.

DR. F. Do you have a girlfriend?

J. No. Not ready to settle down.

DR. F. Where do you live?

J. I have a little house this town gives me, part of the job.

DR. F. And so you're just sort of walking down the street now, kind of keeping an eye on things?

J. Um-hmm.

DR. F. How has the town been? Is it a prosperous town? Small town?

J. It's a small town . . . ah . . . lotta ranch people come in . . . ranch hands and ranch owners, farmers . . . not a lot of people that live in town . . . store owners.

DR. F. Has the town been prospering?

J. It's been growing . . . not much law-breaking here.

DR. J. Are you planning to stay on in this town?

J. I don't think so. It's . . . there's not enough happening . . . the ranch hands get drunk, start shootin' each other . . . and they usually get someone else rather than the person they're shootin' at. Then they think they're good and . . . if it wasn't a fair fight, then they want to shoot it out with me. They're just young kids.

DR. F. What do you do when they want to shoot it out with you?

J. Usually they're not fast at all, and if I'm close I shoot 'em in the knee . . . knocks 'em down. They usually don't even get their gun out of the holster. If I miss the first time . . . then I kill 'em . . . it's not worth them killing me to try to save their life. [His voice heavy with regret.]

DR. F. Now let go of these memories and move ahead to the next significant event. I'm going to count from one to five and on the count of five move ahead in time, perhaps to the event or events that are responsible for your sleeping problem. One . . . two . . . three . . . four . . . five.

J. [Long pause—he frowns as he searches his memory.] It's a larger town . . . I'm a marshal, not a sheriff. It's in Colorado. A lot of saloons in town . . . more gunfighters . . . and . . . drifters . . . people are better with their guns here. They're not like storekeepers and ranch hands. But I like it.

DR. F. You like it here?

J. Um-hmm. [His face becomes animated.] It's exciting.

DR. F. How old are you now?

J. Thirty-two.

DR. F. Tell me what you look like.

J. I'm suntanned . . . my hair is dark . . . and I'm muscular . . . thin hips, waist . . . black boots.

DR. F. I'm going to ask your inner mind to move you ahead to the next significant event. At the count of five. One . . . two . . . three . . . four . . . five.

J. The bank's been robbed.

DR. F. Tell me more about that.

J. It's been robbed by three men . . . and they got away.

DR. F. Did you see it happen?

J. No.

DR. F. When did this happen? What time of day?

J. It was around noon. Someone came to my office and told me.

DR. F. What are you doing now?

J. I'm getting a posse together.

DR. F. How many men will you get?

J. Six or seven.

DR. F. And what do you think your chances are of catching these three robbers?

J. They don't have much of a head start. Not many places they can go.

DR. F. You know the way they headed when they left town?

J. Um-hmm.

DR. F. How do you feel as you're getting these men together?

J. Confident . . . they're just . . . just nothing special.

DR. F. You think you'll catch the bank robbers?

J. Um-hmm.

DR. F. Move ahead and see.

J. We hung 'em. [Indifferently.]

DR. F. I'm going to ask your inner mind to move you
ahead to a very important event at the count of five,
just letting go of these memories. One . . . two . . .
three . . . four . . . five.

J. I'm shooting pool . . . it's at night. Town's fairly
quiet . . . there's two deputies . . . they check the
stores . . . watch the saloons . . . so I'm with
some people, shooting pool.

DR. F. Are you enjoying yourself?

J. Um-hmm.

DR. F. Are you good at pool?

J. Um-hmm . . . and these are nice people, banker
. . . mayor. They all have pool tables at their house.

DR. F. Are you at someone's house?

J. No . . . this . . . the pool hall in town.

DR. F. And you're playing with the banker and the
mayor. Just the three of you?

J. Um-hmm.

DR. F. And now if something happens during this evening, your inner mind will take you to that moment
at the count of five. One . . . two . . . three . . .
four . . . five.

J. [Flinches violently.] Somebody shot me.

DR. F. Somebody shot you?

J. Yeah. Through the open window. At the pool hall.

DR. F. Where did they get you?

J. It was a shotgun . . . across my stomach and in my
chest. [Gasping for breath.]

DR. F. Where are you right now?

J. [His face is contorted with pain.] I'm on the floor.

DR. F. Tell me what you're experiencing.

J. I'm more surprised than anything. It hurts, but not,

172

not that much. I'm just surprised I'd let that happen.

DR. F. What do you mean?

J. That I wasn't . . . is that I would be caught, just . . . for somebody to ambush me. [Anger in his voice and face.]

DR. F. You're surprised that you would be not cautious enough?

J. Yes.

DR. F. What is your usual practice?

J. I walk on the dark side of the street . . . looking around corners before stepping out . . . this was right on the main street.

DR. F. So you're not in the pool hall any longer? You left there?

J. No, the pool hall faces the main street.

DR. F. You were playing pool when this happens?

J. Um-hmm.

DR. F. What are you aware of now?

J. They've carried me to the bed . . . upstairs . . . doctor . . . my stomach hurts. [Beads of sweat break out on his face.]

DR. F. Are you bleeding very much?

J. Um-hmm.

DR. F. Are you conscious and aware?

J. Um-hmm.

DR. F. Tell me more. What else is happening?

J. This is the doctor . . . and a woman that helps him . . . the banker and the mayor . . . one of the deputies . . .

DR. F. Then you don't think you're going to make it?

J. There's no way!

DR. F. Why do you say that, Dale?

J. With a shotgun . . . [Short laugh.] . . . too much in the stomach.

DR. F. What are your thoughts about that? How do you feel about dying?

J. It doesn't . . . it doesn't bother me much. I'm just . . . mad . . . I let someone get me like that!

DR. F. How did it happen that you let them get you? Were you off guard, or what happened?

J. I just didn't expect it.

173

DR. F. So because you didn't expect it, you let your guard down?

J. Um-hmm.

DR. F. If you had expected it, what would you have done? How would you have done it differently?

J. I wouldn't have been in a lighted room with the blinds up . . . I just would have kept alert. Stayed out of buildings. They shoot you coming out of a door. The light's at your back.

DR. F. Is that when it happened, when you were coming out the door?

J. I was shooting pool. He shot through the window. Couldn't miss me.

DR. F. All right, now move ahead a few minutes, and see what's happening. One . . . two . . . three . . . four . . . five . . . what are you experiencing?

J. The doctor's pulling the sheet . . . over my face.

DR. F. Where are you when this happens?

J. I'm still in bed.

DR. F. And what are you experiencing?

J. I knew it was gonna happen . . . I don't feel anything.

DR. F. What can you see from where you are?

J. I can see the doctor . . . his nurse cleaning up his . . . tools, instruments. The banker and the mayor . . . saying they're really sorry about it.

DR. F. What else do you see? What do you see on the bed?

J. Just a bloody sheet . . . and me. [Indifferently.]

DR. F. Are you covered up with the sheet at this point?

J. Yes.

DR. F. Where do you feel you are as you're observing this?

J. I don't know. [Sounding very puzzled.]

DR. F. It's going to become clearer and clearer. I'm going to count from one to three and on the count of three it will be very clear where you are. One . . . two . . . three.

J. [Long pause.] It's like I'm looking through the roof.

DR. F. From what direction?

J. Just from the sky.

DR. F. From the sky you are looking through the roof down into the room?

J. [He nods yes.]

DR. F. You feel as if you can see their expressions and hear what they're saying?

J. [Nods again.]

DR. F. Are you there alone?

J. No, there's two people.

DR. F. And who are they? Do they look familiar?

J. No. One's a woman.

DR. F. Anybody you know?

J. No.

DR. F. What is she wearing? What does she look like?

J. She's got on like a . . . a nightgown.

DR. F. Is she saying anything to you?

J. [Sounding mystified.] No.

DR. F. What is the other person like?

J. He's got on like a suit. Very distinguished-looking. I don't know him.

DR. F. They're there with you?

J. Um-hmm.

DR. F. Just see if you're getting any messages from them or any thoughts.

J. He's got me by the arm . . . but he's not talking to me.

DR. F. Is he looking at you?

J. Um-hmm.

DR. F. And where are you going?

J. They're—they're leading me and like consoling me but . . . not with words. But I know what they mean.

DR. F. How do you feel within yourself right now?

J. I feel good. I . . . feel the lack of anger.

DR. F. You were aware of being angry before, is that what you're saying?

J. Yeah, I've always been angry with people.

DR. F. From this spiritual state, tell me why have you always been angry with people? I'm going to ask you to tell me at the count of three. One . . . two . . . three and what comes to mind?

J. They go through life so unprepared. They're so vulnerable. [Short laugh.] And then *I* get killed!

DR. F. What were the events that have resulted in the sleep problem in your life as Joe? What are the significant events that contributed to that, or caused that? Whatever comes to mind.

J. [Long pause.] Most of my awareness had to be at night, alert . . . someone was always trying to make a name for themselves.

DR. F. In what way?

J. They , . . if they could say they killed me.

DR. F. You had to be alert at night?

J. Um-hmm.

DR. F. Do you feel the Indian attack had anything to do with your sleep problem?

J. Yes, it did . . . they chased me for several days . . . I couldn't sleep at night . . .

DR. F. Did you sleep during the day?

J. No.

DR. F. You just didn't sleep at all, is that it?

J. I'd grab little naps but . . . but only when they were quite a way behind me. When I'd get on a high spot . . .

Out of hypnosis, Joe looked momentarily dazed. Then, slowly, he grinned. "There sure are a lot of parallels!" Leaning towards me in his chair, he eagerly explained, "I didn't tell you before, but shooting is—and has been since I was a kid—my favorite sport." He grinned as he added, "And I'm damn good at it!" Growing serious, he put his hands together, finger to finger, and looked deep in thought. "I'm basically a loner. I don't let people get close. Dale and I have that in common. I mean, when I was Dale I was the same as now." He looked a little sheepish as he admitted, "I have a knack for finding people's weakness—I can really spot them."

I smiled as I remembered him telling me about an error—a slip of the tongue—I had made in the speech he had attended. I nodded in agreement that he did seem to seize upon mistakes and "weaknesses." I sug-

176

gested, "For 'homework,' Joe, notice the weaknesses you spot in other people. I've found we can learn a lot about what we consider weaknesses in ourselves that way." He looked surprised. A guilty grin spread over his face. "Hmm, maybe you're right." As he got up to leave, he flashed a big smile—and at the same time he shook his head slowly in semi-disbelief. "If all that was real, it sure explains my being so alert every night. Hope all that changes." "I hope so, too," I replied. He seemed elated.

A few weeks later, by telephone, Joe filled me in on the results of his past-life regression. The night following our session he went to sleep immediately and slept soundly until morning. The following evening he told his family the "whole story," detail by grisly detail, of his life as Dale Short. When he went to bed he found himself reviewing it in his mind and became so intrigued with the details that it was impossible for him to relax enough to sleep well. But since then he has slept soundly every night—without medication.

He also was delighted to report that he passed his real estate exam!

✖

CHAPTER NINE

"They Call It Kissing!"

The child-like voice did not fit with her attractive but sad Chicano face. Her large black eyes dominated her face. She wore no make-up. Her very wavy, long black hair was parted in the middle and gathered at her neck in an elastic. Overweight by a good thirty pounds, she wore dark clothes to conceal her figure.

Forty-six-year-old Maria blurted out, "Look at me! I'm so fat I can't stand myself anymore. It just makes me madder and madder at myself. My life is a mess. Do you know, there's not *one* single thing I like about me—or my life anymore." With tears welling in her eyes, she said, "I don't have anyone. I've never had anyone. I was married for years—but it wasn't fulfilling. My kids are beautiful. But that's not what I mean. Why can't I love a man? I have given up on that." By now she had covered her eyes with her hands. After a few moments she was more composed. Trying to wipe away the tears, which kept coming, she continued, "Ever since I've been a little kid, it's been the same. I used to get tremendous crushes on guys. Then they would disappoint me in one way or another. Sometimes I think I invent reasons. It *never* worked out."

I saw Maria for six sessions. It became very clear to me that she was in pain—more pain than she admitted even to herself. She blamed her problems on "not having anyone—and being such a tub." Our work brought to the surface the real reason, a complete negation of her sexuality.

The two main relationships in her life, with her husband, Robert, and later a lover, Alfonso, both fizzled. There had been very brief, frantic sexual encounters

178

that left her more depressed than before. "I have never felt fulfilled sexually. I can get mildly aroused in the beginning of a sexual experience but soon I feel nothing. I feel such a sense of failure and dejection." She came to see her conflict as an approach-avoidance. She avoided sex because it was physically painful and degrading. "I always feel used. Even with Alfonso, I feel he used me. I know it doesn't make sense, but that's how I felt." She blushed and lowered her voice, "The sick part is that if I don't feel used—and, worse, if it doesn't physically hurt me, I feel cheated. That's the way it's been."

Her inability to enjoy sex dampened and eventually destroyed not only her relationships, but her self-esteem as well. She was puzzled about her lack of warmth and sharing during sex, since in all other areas of her life these were very strong qualities. As a teenager she was acutely aware of sexuality. "I was scared to death of men. I thought they were all ready to jump on me." Some of her attitudes toward sex and herself as a woman we traced to her childhood when she was reared by her grandmother who was vocally averse to all things sexual and actively deprecating of femininity. But this only skimmed the surface of our understanding of this major problem.

During one of our sessions, Maria commented on her frustrations. A recurrent theme in her litany was her feeling of being a nobody—a nothing, having no importance. "I never feel like people are taking me seriously. People don't listen to me because I sound like a little girl." Grinning a little, she related several incidents that illustrated this. Once when sending a telegram the operator congratulated her for "doing such a nice job for such a little girl." Several times a telephone operator had asked to speak to someone older in the household to authorize a collect call. Although she laughed while recalling these events, there was also a heavy note—a sense of worthlessness and frustration.

Another problem that emerged during our work together was Maria's rebelliousness. This became increasingly apparent as she struggled to stay on the diet and meditation program we had worked out together during our first session. Rebelliousness also seemed very incompatible with the rest of her personality. It didn't fit with the responsibility she carried so well in her work with people—with her superior intelligence and maturity. As she put it, "It's totally at odds with my goals of losing weight, trying to solve my problems and learning to relax by meditating." I wondered about these two discrepancies, the child-like voice and her rebelliousness. I filed them away as something we might learn about through our hypnotic work.

During one of our sessions, under hypnosis, Maria's inner mind indicated that her problems with sex originated in an event from a former lifetime. The setting seemed to be Arabian. I regressed her to that event.

DR. F. What are you experiencing?

M. [Silence. Shakes her head no.]

DR. F. You're shaking your head no.

M. I don't like what I see. [Her voice becomes even more child-like.]

DR. F. Just speak out whatever comes to your mind.

M. I belong to someone.

DR. F. Yes?

M. I was brought to a room. There were a lot of men there. Oh, I don't want to do this! [Tears beginning to form.]

DR. F. Do you know who you are?

M. [Weeping.] It's almost like I'm nobody.

DR. F. About how old are you?

M. Nine.

DR. F. What is your name?

M. Phillepa.

DR. F. What country are you from, Phillepa?

M. I don't understand "country."

DR. F. That's all right. Tell me what you're experiencing Phillepa. Who's taking you into the room?

M. I was sent there.

DR. F. Did you go in by yourself?

M. [Nods yes.]

DR. F. Who sent you?

M. The one who *owns* me.

DR. F. Who is that?

M. An *ugly* man.

DR. F. Are the men in there his friends?

M. No . . . no! Not friends. Just men. I think they're businessmen . . . he's some kind of merchant. I don't know what he does.

DR. F. How many are there?

M. [Looking around.] Eleven.

DR. F. Do you know what's going to happen?

M. It happened before. [Becoming upset.]

DR. F. What happens?

M. [Silence.]

DR. F. Tell me what happens.

M. [Whispered.] I don't want to know.

DR. F. Become calm and relaxed. I'm going to count to five. With each count you will feel more and more relaxed. One . . . two . . . three . . . four . . . five.

M. [Long pause.] I have feelings and . . . I think things . . . but everyone acts as if I shouldn't, as if I don't . . . I just belong to someone . . . and they can send me here and they can send me there, "Do this and do that" . . . they don't believe that I have a right. But I do.

DR. F. You know that you have a right, but they don't know that.

M. They say I don't.

DR. F. Who are they?

M. All the people. The one I belong to and the people who come . . . they don't even act like I exist—I'm a *thing*.

DR. F. What kinds of things do you have to do? Do you do housework and that kind of thing?

M. That's not the part. That's not the part that's bad. It's the sexual part that is bad . . . I could die and they don't care.

DR. F. You're nothing to them?

M. I was born—they don't care.

DR. F. How did it come that this man owned you? Where are your parents?

181

M. I don't remember. It's just like I was there.

DR. F. It's the sexual part that really bothers you, not the housework?

M. I don't do much housework.

DR. F. What do you generally do?

M. I get up in the morning and I go down to get something to eat . . . there's no warmth, the place is always cold, stone floors . . . I'm not supposed to do anything, I'm just told to stay out of the way.

DR. F. Who tells you that?

M. The women who are cooking.

DR. F. Are they aware of the fact that you're used sexually?

M. Um-hmm. That's what I'm there for.

DR. F. Is that the custom in your village?

M. I don't know "custom."

DR. F. How long have you been used this way?

M. . . . A long time.

DR. F. For many years?

M. I don't know "years," but long time.

DR. F. Were you there when you were just a little girl?

M. I don't remember any other place.

DR. F. And now are you ready to go into that room and tell me what happens?

M. [Long silence.]

DR. F. Now it's very, very important for you to go back through this even though it's not pleasant. It will free you to know. And now I want you to enter the room and tell me what happens.

M. [Long silence.]

DR. F. What's happening now?

M. I know what to do.

DR. F. And what is that?

M. There's lots of feelings.

DR. F. What are those feelings?

M. It's . . . it's exciting . . . [Her face becomes animated.] . . . and it's painful . . . [Frowning.] . . . but there's something that I feel about it, but at the same time makes me feel bad about . . . it's that I'm not *real* for them.

DR. F. Tell me more.

M. I don't really understand . . . should I tell you? [Weeping.]

DR. F. I think it would be very helpful for you to.

M. It's *terrible!*

DR. F. I'm sure it is.

M. [Sobbing.] I don't even think you want to know.

DR. F. I want to help you. I think that your knowing about it will help you very, very much.

M. Then I will say it. [Trying to wipe away the tears.] I go to each man, that's what they've trained me to do. [She starts sobbing again.]

DR. F. They've trained you to go to each man . . .

M. It's like a greeting and I greet them.

DR. F. In what manner?

M. They think it's so funny. [With contempt on her face.]

DR. F. Are they dressed?

M. Yes.

DR. F. Are you also dressed?

M. I have a white gown on that I put on special for this. I don't have anything under it. I go to each man and I undress him, not all . . . of him, and . . . then . . . [Lowering her voice.] . . . they call it kissing! They think it's so funny.

DR. F. How do you feel about what you have to do?

M. There's some pleasure in it, but not the way they make me do it.

DR. F. What do you mean by that?

M. I don't mind doing it, it's that they don't see that I'm a person . . . they don't care how *I* feel. So while I'm . . . I'm scared . . . I'm mad at them, but I feel horrible. What I feel is anger too . . . [Brightening up.] . . . do you know, I think I know I don't have to do this. They tell me to, but I don't have to do this and so I do it because I want to. [Amazement in her voice.]

DR. F. You've been brought up on this and been trained to do this, isn't that right? This is also one way for you to get attention. Did you ever think of that?

M. No.

DR. F. Do you get much attention otherwise?

M. I'm just told to stay out of the way . . . until I'm told I have to come.

DR. F. Is your owner there too with the other men?

M. Um-hmm. And all the time I'm doing this, I'm thinking about them . . . and I'm thinking that I'm enjoying it, they don't think I'm enjoying it and so . . . so it's almost like I'm tricking them . . . 'cuz I'm not supposed to feel anything. I'm supposed to be a thing. And so I think, they don't think I'm anything, but I'm tricking! . . . That's how I feel sometimes, like I can laugh at them. But still, these funny feelings . . . like right now all I can feel is they're stupid!

DR. F. Tell me what else happens.

M. See I feel better when I think they're stupid. 'Cuz if I don't feel they're stupid . . . then I feel like I'm nothing . . . and I'm being used.

DR. F. What happens next, after the greeting?

M. This time I don't do what they usually want. [Defiantly.].

DR. F. What is that?

M. This time I laugh at them. [She spits out the words.] This time I tell them they're stupid.

DR. F. Go on.

M. This is where I feel better 'cuz I know I don't *have* to do this anymore. I don't *have* to . . . and now I don't want to and . . . and I'm not going to. [Whispering.]

DR. F. How do they react to that?

M. [Smiling.] My owner's angry.

DR. F. You're smiling.

M. Yes. He's angry 'cuz he looks like a fool in front of his . . . these men . . . and I'm gonna show him. And I think, that's all right with me!

DR. F. What is it that they usually have you do?

M. They use their little games where they have me come and and . . . and I greet them, what the stupids call "kissing," the dirty old men! . . . [Her voice shakes with emotion.] And then they just put me on the table in the middle of the room and they just all do anything they want to . . . one by one . . . and the rest stand around . . . and watch.

DR. F. So you're not going to do that this time?

M. Nope, 'cuz I don't have to.

DR. F. What does your owner say or do?

M. He's really mad . . . that's okay with me . . . I think he's going to kill me . . . but that's okay with me . . . I'd like that better. I have to do it.

DR. F. What makes you think he's going to kill you or wants to kill you?

M. If I don't do what he wants me to, that's the only thing I do. I don't do anything else.

DR. F. You have a very satisfied and happy look on your face.

M. I feel that way . . . I don't *have* to do it. I don't want to and the most he can do is kill me. He can't hurt me anymore . . . he has told me that I am not a person, that I don't exist. They don't . . . they haven't said this, you know, but this is what they're . . . this is their attitude. And so I'm just saying that's not true.

DR. F. Tell me what you say to them. Tell me your exact words.

M. I stand up on the table and I'm saying, "You're all stupid! You think I don't have any feelings. You think I'm just something like the table and the only ones that are important are you and what you feel and what you think . . . You're more concerned with how the other person, the other men think about you than what *I* think of you. And all the time I *am* thinking and I'm thinking how silly you are, how stupid you are, how ugly you are because *I'm* the one that's using you because I don't think you have any minds at all." [Lowering her voice.] They think I'm crazy.

DR. F. How do you know that? What do they say?

M. They're talkin' about me.

DR. F. What are they saying about you?

M. Just lookin' at each other and they're saying, "She's gone insane!"

DR. F. What does your owner say?

M. He just said, "That's all right. There's another one." Now I don't feel so good because there's another

185

one . . . that means some other little girl's gonna have to do this.

DR. F. Is that the part that really bothers you or does it bother you because you're not special?

M. [Her voice heavy with dejection.] Maybe. They just dismissed me. So I lost after all. I don't care.

DR.F. Did you really lose? You stood up for your rights and you didn't do what you didn't want to do, did you? That doesn't sound like losing to me.

M. Yes, but you see, if they get it from me or they get it from someone else it makes no difference to them. They didn't hear what I said to them . . . do you know, I think I'm an old lady 'cuz sometimes I wonder, how come I think this way?

DR. F. Do you feel like an old lady with all your wisdom, is that what you're saying?

M. How come I think this way? And they're older than I am.

DR. F. But inside you feel older than they?

M. [Nods her head yes.]

DR. F. Then what happens after you are on the table? Do you get down from the table?

M. The old man says, "Get out!" And I just wonder, can it be that easy? I think they're afraid of me. And now I'm afraid because . . . what am I going to do now?

DR. F. And what happens next?

M. They won't let me stay in the house anymore. [Her whole body starts to tremble.]

DR. F. Who is "they"?

M. The women.

DR. F. Are they angry with you?

M. I think they're afraid. They think I'm crazy. Maybe I am.

DR. F. You don't sound crazy to me. You just sound like a little girl who stood up for her rights and who didn't want to be considered a nonentity, a nonperson.

M. Don't I sound like an old lady?

DR. F. You do. Maybe you have some inner wisdom, but that doesn't make you crazy. Now I'd like to go ahead to the next significant event. I'm going to count from one to five. One . . . two . . . three . . . four . . . five.

M. [Long silence.]

DR. F. What are you experiencing?

M. [Smiling.] I'm not dead and I'm surprised.

DR. F. Where are you?

M. I don't really know. I've never been outside the house.

DR. F. Look around and describe what you see.

M. I think I went out and sat on a wall that was white. I was sitting there with my head in my hands, just sitting there. I thought they were going to kill me and they didn't . . . just sitting there and . . . and what I think now . . . [Flinching.] . . . someone came up behind me and . . . and cut my head off!

DR. F. So you were killed after all, but you didn't realize it?

M. I can feel it . . . [Putting her hand to the back of her neck.]

DR. F. Tell me what you saw.

M. I'm sitting there and . . . yet I'm out here and . . . I can see it. The little girl never knew it, but somebody came up behind her with a big knife and just cut her head off. She never knew it . . . she still thinks she's thinking.

DR. F. I'd like you to return to the present, Maria . . . staying deeply relaxed. At the count of zero you will be back to September, 1976. Ten . . . nine . . . eight . . . seven . . . six . . . five . . . four . . . three . . . two . . . one . . . zero. Tell me about the little girl. What was her life like?

M. Well, it was very much of an empty life. There wasn't much to do. She didn't really have anything she had to do, no tasks, you know. She wasn't required to sew or anything. She was just there . . . almost like . . . like a puppy or a kitten doesn't have a thing to do. All they have to do is be there in case someone wants to pet them. And that was it. All the women would feed her, but just tell her, "Just stay out of my way."

187

DR. F. Now what happened to her in the end?

M. Well, she was wondering how come she had left that room because she thought for sure that she was going to be killed . . . and then went out and sat down and was thinking, I was going to die, and . . . then it's almost like I could see she was sitting there still thinking and then someone came up behind her and he cut her head off.

When she came out of hypnosis, she began weeping silently. She took a few minutes to compose herself. After drying her tears with a Kleenex, she looked at me and with emotion in her voice said, "What a sad little thing I was." Shuddering, she continued, "They were such ugly men. No wonder I'm not very trusting." She got up to leave. Then she turned to me, "Thank you for that. I would have never known. And I need to know."

When Maria came in for our next session, she seemed lighter and happier. Yet her mood quickly altered as she became lost in thought. She looked back on her regression as Phillepa. She said, "I still feel like that little girl. I know now, at a gut level, why I turned off all my sexual feelings. No wonder I can't give sexually. Now I understand why I saw men as lechers." She also clearly knew why she had the need for and aversion to pain, being used and degradation. She could *feel* Phillepa's rebelliousness and knew it was the same feeling she always had when required to do something. We both felt that her child-like voice was a vestige of Phillepa, symbolizing what a powerful influence that part of her had on her entire being.

Under hypnosis Maria's subconscious mind indicated by her finger signals that she had had many incarnations as a woman. She disclosed that she had never been a woman in a sexual sense since her lifetime of sexual abuse as Phillepa. While still deeply hypnotized, she traveled back to one life as a priestess and another as a medicine woman in Arizona. In both she devoted herself to spirituality and healing. However, even in her life as a priestess, she had tragedy associated with love and a sexual experience. I regressed her to that lifetime. She became tense and said:

M. I'm in the Yucatan . . . I wasn't supposed to love him.

DR. F. Why is that?

M. Because I was a priestess and I couldn't believe in love. I had to do something more important and . . . and he kept bothering me by being there.

DR. F. Who is he?

M. [Very upset, difficulty in breathing.] A soldier. [Turning her head to the side, as though seeing someone.] You lie when you say you love me! . . . [Turning back to me.] I loved him and he kept coming and . . . and I think someone found out . . . I think he must have killed us. [She covers her eyes with her hands.]

DR. F. Were you killed because of your love for him?

M. No. [Very agitated.]

DR. F. Did you have sex with him?

M. Oh, I'm not comfortable! . . . I had sex with him . . . because he talked me into it!

DR. F. Were you killed because you had sex?

M. [Tears are streaming down her cheeks.] Yes . . . they threw me into that pool. [Pointing.]

Maria and I will work together for only two more sessions. The child-like voice is still with us. The pounds are giving way to a diet. It's not easy for her, because Mexican food is part of her life. However, she is learning to be aware of calories and good nutrition for the first time in her life. She no longer eats out of anxiety, boredom and depression—but because she enjoys food.

Maria is now a happy person. She is bursting with energy and is starting many new projects. The most exciting one is a trip to Arizona. "I feel pulled to go there. Do you think it will seem like home to me?" she asked. Another is changing her image. She is looking around for a good hair stylist, because she wants to wear her

189

hair very short—to show off her mass of curls. And lately she's been wearing a trace of make-up.

She now has fantasies about "Mr. Right" coming into her life. She has hopes—dreams.

Maria has freed herself from the centuries-old subconscious memories that had robbed her of her natural birthright—sexual expression.

❈

CHAPTER TEN

"It Cost Me My Life!"

"All my life, as far back as I can remember, I've had problems making decisions." Roger looked embarrassed. His voice was soft, and hesitant. "It doesn't matter if they are small decisions or important ones, I always find myself *agonizing* over them."

Roger was a handsome, tall, dark-haired man in his mid-thirties. The clothes he was wearing were obviously imported and top quality: flawlessly tailored, brown French slacks, an elegant print shirt, well-polished cordovan boots. Even his cologne suggested a French label. His brown eyes changed expression from moment to moment, as he painted a picture of a man constantly in a state of vacillation—often immobilized. "I'm impulsive —that way I force myself to act—sometimes—no, often —not wisely." He gave example after example of the range and variety of decisions that had become insurmountable obstacles. His body, as well as his words, expressed frustration, helplessness, irritation, confusion and downright anger—directed at himself. He sighed deeply as he explained that this problem had been a major reason why he had stayed in an unrewarding marriage for over a decade. He finally got out of it. The decision was made for him. Now his biggest concern was whether or not to end a thirteen-year career as a college instructor and pursue one as a filmmaker.

In a matter-of-fact tone of voice he continued to describe himself. His indecisiveness didn't fit with the rest of his characteristics. When he did something, he did it well. His classes were among the most popular, his rating by his students extremely favorable. The few films he had produced were highly praised by fellow filmmakers. He excelled in any project or interest he pursued.

He came to me because hypnosis was a last resort. He had dabbled in many therapies, ranging from Reichian therapy to Transactional Analysis—even marathon encounter groups. "Hypnosis might very well reveal something going on at a subconscious level," I agreed. "If so, it could help you assess an issue, make a positive, well-thought-out decision and act upon it." Roger smiled and said, "Maybe I can get rid of my headaches and back problems. Wouldn't that be something?"

Roger proved an excellent hypnotic subject. His whole body relaxed as he closed his eyes. His breathing became slow and regular. He established clear, fast finger signals without difficulty. His subconscious mind made it clear that there were *six* events from *six* past lifetimes that were responsible for his problem.

I asked his inner mind to prepare him at a subconscious level to look at these events the next time we met. Just before ending our first session, he brightened up and enthusiastically exclaimed, "If I get this problem solved, there'll be no stopping me!"

About ten days later, Roger came for his next appointment. He arrived a good ten minutes early. After waiting, he came into the room and quickly settled himself into the reclining chair. He smiled and said, "I'm ready. I hope it works."

He closed his eyelids and began concentrating on his breathing. His eyes rolled up. His eyelids fluttered. He was already in a trance. I deepened his level and proceeded with the regression. I suggested his inner mind take him back to one of the six events from the past that were responsible for his problem. I counted him back in time and asked him what he was aware of:

R. [Hesitantly.] I was at a . . . carnival.
DR. F. Are you still there?
R. No.
DR. F. What are you aware of?
R. I'm not sure if it's a carnival. It's some kind of big doings.
DR. F. Tell me about it. What was it like?

R. Maybe a jousting contest.

DR. F. I'd like you to go back to that. I'm going to count from one to three and you will go back. One . . . two . . . three. What are you experiencing?

R. Confusion.

DR. F. You will receive very vivid impressions at the count of three. One . . . two . . . three. Now, what are you aware of?

R. Well, it was . . . lot of colorful tents . . . a few colorful tents on a . . . green with people . . . walking about.

DR. F. What are the people wearing?

R. Some are dressed elegantly and others are not.

DR. F. What is the style of their clothing?

R. Well, some, like the monks, are draped in . . . in a kind of brown smock with hoods and other people are dressed in a . . . I'd say, sort of bright pantaloons and very colorful regalia and others are dressed in very common clothes with nubby-textured, handmade wool and so on.

DR. F. And what is the occasion?

R. I believe . . . yes, it's a jousting contest.

DR. F. Can you see the people who are jousting?

R. Hmm . . . no, I can't now.

DR. F. Is it over? Is that why you can't see it?

R. Well, ah . . . I have the feeling *I'm* going to be in it . . . and I have to select a . . . a . . . either a club with a—with a ball on it on a chain or an ax.

DR. F. And which are you going to select? Which do you usually use?

R. I usually use the club with the ball and chain with the points on the ball . . . but I think I selected the ax.

DR. F. What made you decide to select the ax?

R. I thought it would be better.

DR. F. And you've already made a selection, is that it?

R. Um-hmm.

DR. F. Where are you at this moment?

R. I'm in a tent waiting for my ah . . . turn. [His voice trembles.]

DR. F. And what are you doing?

R. I'm just waiting.

DR. F. Are you standing or sitting?

R. I'm sitting and I'm in my ah . . . I'm sitting on a horse in my armor.

DR. F. Tell me about yourself. How old are you?

R. Nineteen.

DR. F. What's your name?

R. William.

DR. F. What's your last name, William?

R. William of Orr . . . William of something like that.

DR. F. I'm going to count from one to three and at the end of the count you will know exactly what your name is. One . . . two . . . three and what comes to mind?

R. I think it's William of Orr.

DR. F. Is Orr the town that you live in, William?

R. I think it's the county . . . or something.

DR. F. Do you enjoy jousting?

R. I do, yes.

DR. F. What is this occasion?

R. It's a . . . in order to—it's like a tryout to be a knight.

DR. F. I see. And if you're a knight, can you tell me what that would mean to you?

R. [Proudly.] You would be given in service to your king.

DR. F. And who is your king?

R. Henry . . . it's King Henry of England.

DR. F. What's the year now, William?

R. Fourteen . . . I think it's fourteen eighty-six. [Remembering English history, he would be Henry VII.]

DR. F. How do you feel as you're waiting there, William?

R. [Beads of sweat forming on his face.] I'm—I'm a little bit nervous.

DR. F. How can you tell you're nervous? What happens to you?

R. My stomach is a . . . I can feel my stomach is—is—feels like a—a—a . . . is churning and it's a . . . very warm . . . and I feel like I'm . . . a little bit like I might throw up.

DR. F. Have you ever had these feelings before?

R. Feel hot inside.

DR. F. Hot inside your body?

R. In my stomach.

DR. F. How does the armor feel on your body?

R. It gives me a good, secure feeling.

DR. F. What do you have on your head?

R. [Touching his head.] I have a helmet.

DR. F. Is there any part of you that's exposed, that could be hurt by the other opponent?

R. Well, he can puncture any of it.

DR. F. He can puncture the armor?

R. With a lance.

DR. F. Do you know what weapon your opponent will be using?

R. I think he's going to have a . . . [Deep sigh.] We both have the same. A lance and another.

DR. F. What are the rules of jousting? If you had picked the other weapon, the ax, would your opponent also have to use the ax?

R. I'm not sure . . . I think so.

DR. F. Now I'm going to count from one to three and on the count of three, you will know. You'll know all about the rules of jousting. One . . . two . . . three and what comes to mind?

R. [With sureness.] If I have an ax, he gets a club or vice versa.

DR. F. Who gets to make the first choice? How is that decided?

R. We picked sticks.

DR. F. Go on.

R. The longest one chooses.

DR. F. In this case who picked the longest?

R. I did.

DR. F. Are you glad about that? Is it important to be able to make that choice?

R. I . . . it could be.

DR. F. Now, tell me about yourself as you're waiting, William. Do you live with your family?

R. They live on a farm and I live in town.

DR. F. Do you live by yourself or do you live with someone?

R. I've been given into service to my . . . lord.

DR. F. And how do you feel about that?

R. I'm proud to have been picked.

DR. F. Were there many young men who were candidates?

R. Not as strong or as big as I. [Said with obvious pride—and a smile.]

DR. F. How big are you?

R. [Silence.]

DR. F. Do you know how tall you are?

R. Three sticks or something like that.

DR. F. I'm going to count from one to three and you will know. One . . . two . . . three and what comes to mind?

R. They measure you by sticks—a stick. I don't know what it is. But it's a stick and I'm three sticks tall.

DR. F. Is that quite a bit taller than most people?

R. Umm—yes. I'm about a head taller than most.

DR. F. What is your body like?

R. It's a—I'm tall and . . . and . . . and muscular, but not fat.

DR. F. All right, now. I'm going to ask you to go to the next significant event at the count of five. Just let go of these memories. One . . . two . . . three . . . four . . . five and what comes to mind?

R. I'm in the chute.

DR. F. Tell me how you feel.

R. I feel a warmth . . . a nervousness, throughout my body.

DR. F. What are you thinking?

R. [Rubbing his hands nervously.] I just want to get it over. I just want to win!

DR. F. Now I'm going to count from one to three and on the count of three you will be at the next significant event. One . . . two . . . three and what comes to mind?

R. [His body jerks strongly.] I got knocked off my horse by my opponent's lance.

DR. F. Where are you now?

R. I'm in—in—in the green.

DR. F. You're standing or are you down on the ground?

R. No, I had—I got up.

DR. F. And now what happens?

R. He's still on his horse.

DR. F. How do you feel?

R. Ah . . . I feel more ashamed than I am scared, but . . . [Long pause, his voice becoming slurred.] . . . I am kind of disoriented.

DR. F. Is that because of the way you landed?

R. I think my stomach is injured.

DR. F. And now what happens?

R. He's a . . . trying to get behind me . . . circle around behind me and . . . attack me with his club.

DR. F. Is he able to stay on his horse?

R. Yes, he can move faster than I can . . . and I'm trying to maneuver away from him.

DR. F. Now what is he doing? Just describe it.

R. He keeps circling around trying to get behind me.

DR. F. Are you standing up?

R. Partially.

DR. F. And now what happens?

R. He keeps trying to circle around behind me and then charge in from behind and . . . [Dodging.] . . . club me with his club. I try to—hack—hack at him with my ax, but he's on his horse and it's hard to get him with an ax.

DR. F. If you had picked the other weapon, how would that have been?

R. I could have pulled him—I could have wrenched him off his horse with—wrapping it around his neck.

DR. F. What are you thinking now—about the choice of weapons?

R. I would have been better off with the club.

DR. F. You feel you made a poor choice?

R. [Nodding.] I definitely made a poor choice.

DR. F. Now what are you doing?

R. I think he ran me down with his horse and . . . and clubbed me with his . . . clubbed me in the head with his—with his—with his club. [His face is in agony.]

197

DR. F. Where are you?

R. [His voice fading.] I'm lying there in the green.

DR. F. How do you feel?

R. [Silence.]

DR. F. What are you aware of?

R. I just feel nothing . . . just kind of a warmth and a . . . kind of like blood . . . red blood, a warm blood is running through my body . . . and I'm just . . . kind of . . . I saw a white light and . . . I just kind of floated away.

Since he did not seem exhausted from our work so far, I asked his subconscious mind to take him to another of the events we needed to look at. After some initial resistance, he commented, "The word 'Germany' came to mind." He spoke of a feeling of "uneasiness" along his spinal cord. We worked through more resistance and finally broke through. After a long pause, he finally said:

R. I can see, ah . . . German uniforms, ah . . . officers' uniforms . . . and I have the impression that I was a colonel in the SS.

DR. F. What is your name?

R. [Silence.]

DR. F. Whatever comes to mind at the count of three. One . . . two . . . three.

R. I have the impression of "Karl."

DR. F. Karl, what is your last name?

R. Heinman or something like that.

DR. F. What are you doing right now, Karl?

R. [Long pause.] I think I'm . . . I . . . I'm hanging!

DR. F. You're hanging?

R. I was hanged by a wire.

DR. F. Tell me more about that.

R. I can feel it . . . pulling on my neck. [Putting his hands to his neck.]

DR. F. Was this an accident?

R. No.

DR. F. Tell me more about it. What are you experiencing?

R. [Deep sigh.] Ah . . . I—I—I was suspected of not having—of having divided loyalties toward Hitler . . . and I was beaten . . . and then tortured . . . stripped and hanged . . . hanged by the neck with a wire . . . and photographed.

DR. F. Why were you photographed?

R. As an example to others . . . ah . . . my staff was forced to watch me be hanged . . . [Becoming agitated.]

DR. F. Stay calm and relaxed . . . calm and very relaxed. Tell me what you're experiencing.

R. [Relaxing a little.] Well, what I was experiencing was my hatred toward the bureaucratic red tape and the—the politics in the German army . . . and ah . . . I felt you couldn't be a good German and you couldn't be a good . . . soldier in that structure.

DR. F. Now, let go of those memories. Just concentrate on your breathing. Your inner mind will take you back to the event responsible for your problem in your current lifetime. I'm going to count from one to five. One . . . two . . . three . . . four . . . five and what comes to mind?

R. I'm at a meeting of high-ranking officers . . . in Berlin.

DR. F. What is the purpose of the meeting?

R. They were discussing the stupidity of . . . Hitler's stupidity and . . . and how he's going to . . . to lose the war for Germany.

DR. F. And what are you saying?

R. I can just feel the tightness on my vocal cords. I don't seem to be saying anything.

DR. F. What else are you aware of?

R. I am very proud of my uniform and my country . . . and my affiliation with the SS—my position.

DR. F. What are you experiencing?

R. I feel a lot of emotion in my body . . . but I can't see anything.

DR. F. At the count of five it will become very, very clear to you. You will become calmer and calmer

with each count. One . . . two . . . three . . .
four . . . five. What comes to mind?

R. I'm at a council.

DR. F. Tell me more about that.

R. There's a . . . three officers that I admire. I think
they're generals or colonels. One of them is a general.
He has a red stripe on a gray uniform.

DR. F. What are you doing there?

R. I just nodded my approval.

DR. F. Of what?

R. A plan to kill Hitler.

DR. F. Are there just four of you there?

R. There's five of us at the meeting. I think seven are
involved . . . or more than five.

DR. F. There are seven?

R. Two, not at the meeting.

DR. F. Tell me more. What are you planning? How are
you planning to kill him?

R. Hitler, with a bomb.

DR. F. How?

R. Plant a bomb in a—in a . . . plane or a bunker
. . . close to Hitler.

DR. F. Whose idea was that?

R. A colonel with a . . . a . . . one eye—patch on
his eye.

DR. F. And do you think it's a good idea?

R. It must be done!

DR. F. Why is that?

R. To save Germany and . . . take control of the war
for the . . . fighting men that have died.

DR. F. Is that the decision that your inner mind consid-
ers a poor decision in terms of its outcome for you?
If it is, your "yes" finger will lift and if it isn't, your
"no" finger will lift.

R. ["No" finger lifts.]

DR. F. Was there another decision that you made that
was a poor one?

R. I think the poor decision was to enter a conspiracy of
so many people . . . I think that was the real mistake.

DR. F. Was that the real mistake?

R. That's the mistake that led to my . . . demise.

DR. F. Tell me how you feel about that.

R. You can't trust that many people . . . their loyalties change from day to day under stress.

DR. F. Tell me how you were found out. At the count of three. One . . . two . . . three and what comes to mind?

R. Someone talked . . . someone was tortured.

DR. F. Someone was tortured and talked?

R. Um-hmm. Plan failed.

DR. F. And then what happened?

R. We were all rounded up.

DR. F. Where were you when they caught you?

R. I was in my office.

DR. F. What year is it?

R. Nineteen forty.

DR. F. Tell me what happened.

R. They came in and . . . they beat me over my table—over my desk with the butts of rifles . . . broke my back . . . paralyzed.

DR. F. Is that what you remembered at first?

R. That's how they beat me. And then they strung me . . . up later . . . naked with a—a—strangled me with a wire around my neck . . . but I may have been dead already . . . with—in a room with other people . . . with everybody forced to watch.

DR. F. All right, I'm going to ask your inner mind to just let go of all those memories. And now take you to another lifetime—another lifetime in which there is some event that is in some way related to your problem with indecisiveness. I'm going to ask your inner mind to take you to that event at the count of ten. One . . . two . . . three . . . [Continues to count.] Where are you now?

R. Ah . . . mountain.

DR. F. You're on a mountain?

R. The base of the mountain. It's snow-covered.

DR. F. Who are you?

R. [Long pause.]

DR. F. At the count of three you will know. One . . . two . . . three.

R. I think I'm an Indian or a . . . a Tibetan tribesman or something . . . small.

DR. F. Tell me more about yourself.

R. My name is Tanakee . . . I'm a small, burly, kind of powerful man.

DR. F. How old are you?

R. Nineteen.

DR. F. What kind of work do you do?

R. I think I'm a peasant. I work in the fields.

DR. F. What are you doing right at this moment, Tanakee?

R. Standing, looking up at the mountain.

DR. F. What do you think of when you look up at that mountain?

R. Well, someone's talking to me about climbing the mountain . . . or help them climb the mountain . . . carry their things.

DR. F. Who is talking about that?

R. A foreigner. A Swiss, I think.

DR. F. Have you ever gone up the mountain before?

R. No!

DR. F. How do you feel as he's talking about this to you?

R. [Frowning.] It's dangerous and it's against my values!

DR. F. Can you tell me more about that?

R. You don't go above . . . our village.

DR. F. Why is that?

R. It's too dangerous. [With awe in his voice.]

DR. F. When you said it's against your values, what did you mean?

R. It's a rule of our village.

DR. F. Why is it a rule of your village?

R. [Lowering his voice.] Too many have died on the mountain.

DR. F. Is there a name for this mountain?

R. We have a name . . . but they call it something else.

DR. F. What do you call it?

R. The Terrible One.

DR. F. Why do you call it the Terrible One?

R. Because of the winds—terrific winds that come off it . . . the cold winds that come off of the mountain . . . vast and forbidding.

DR. F. Tell me more.

R. It's too big . . . and too dangerous to climb.

DR. F. This man is talking to you about going up on the mountain?

R. Carrying their things to a base camp.

DR. F. Is he talking to you alone or to others also?

R. Twenty-nine people in the village.

DR. F. How do you feel about it?

R. I want to go.

DR. F. Why is that?

R. I think it's a challenge and it's . . . a lot of money.

DR. F. How much money are they going to pay you?

R. Something per day. Fifty cents a day. That's a lot of money, more than we could make.

DR. F. How do the others feel about going?

R. They're excited. We're all excited about the challenge and about making . . . the money.

DR. F. What do you do or say?

R. Hmm. I think I'm just going along with them.

DR. F. Tell me more about what you're observing.

R. Well, I can see the village. A lot of people gathering together and . . . talking of this.

DR. F. Are the foreigners still there with you?

R. They're . . . off to the side, to the left of us . . . waiting for an answer. There's terrific excitement and stirring. People wondering if we will go and . . . talking about what might happen if we should go.

DR. F. Do you say anything?

R. I'm not a leader.

DR. F. But you want to go?

R. I want to go.

DR. F. What is the decision?

R. [With excitement in his voice—his body.] We're going to go!

DR. F. And now I'm going to ask you to go to the next significant event at the count of five. Just let go of these memories. One . . . two . . . three . . . four . . . five and what comes to mind?

R. The climbing with great . . . packs on our backs . . . huge weight on our backs . . . and across the ice.

DR. F. What are you wearing?

R. I'm wearing warm clothes . . . [Frowning.] . . . but my feet are cold.

DR. F. Is the rest of your body warm?

R. I have a hat and jacket and long, warm pants . . . and my feet are . . . very cold. Freezing cold!

DR. F. Is it just your feet that are cold?

R. And my hands. [Rubbing them.]

DR. F. How are your legs and arms? Are they warm?

R. They're warm. My head is warm . . . my face is burned from the . . . sun.

DR. F. Does it hurt?

R. It's parched and it hurts.

DR. F. Have you been climbing for long?

R. For three days.

DR. F. Tell me more about how you feel. Are you still glad that you're doing this?

R. I think I'm excited but . . . tired.

DR. F. All right. And now I'm going to ask you to move to the next event of significance—a very important event at the count of five. One . . . two . . . three . . . four . . . five and what comes to mind? Stay calm and relaxed, very calm and very relaxed.

R. We have to walk across a bridge . . . an ice bridge . . . ah . . . on a . . . and, ahhh—[Trembling violently.] As we did, it broke and . . . and three of us fell in.

DR. F. Into what?

R. A deep crevasse and I . . . I was killed.

DR. F. Can you see that happening?

R. I can see that happening. All three of us going . . . falling, because we were roped together. I was pulled backwards. I was across . . . but pulled backwards. [Breathing very fast.]

DR. F. Become calm and relaxed . . . very calm . . . very relaxed.

R. [His body relaxes considerably, breathing is slower.]

DR. F. Was there any decision-making about going across

that ice bridge or was it something that just had to be done?

R. I think I wanted to go back, but I didn't want to . . . but we were kind of forced to go.

DR. F. And now I'm going to ask your inner mind at the count of three to give you insight about what it is, which incident is related to your problem of making decisions in this lifetime. One . . . two . . . three and what comes to mind?

R. I think that I didn't follow my own judgment.

DR. F. What was your own judgment?

R. To go back . . . but I wouldn't—I didn't assert myself.

DR. F. You wanted to go back to your village, is that it?

R. I wanted to go back when my feet were freezing . . . but I didn't assert myself.

DR. F. Your inner mind will indicate if that is the incident that is related to your problem up here in 1977.

R. ["Yes" finger lifts instantly.]

DR. F. The fact that you did not go back after you got going and your feet were cold—you wanted to go back and you didn't?

R. ["Yes" finger lifts again.]

DR. F. Tell me more about the decision.

R. I think I made the decision to go on rather than to assert myself . . . to speak up.

DR. F. All right now. Are there any other decisions . . . ?

R. The other decision is that I don't want to cross the ice and I'm standing there. We talked about it . . . and I'm the first to go.

DR. F. You didn't want to go?

R. No.

DR. F. Why did you go?

R. Well, because I was bulldozed by the others . . . by two others.

DR. F. Is that one of the decisions also that is responsible for this problem up here in this lifetime?

R. ["Yes" finger.]

DR. F. Are there any other problems from that life that

affected you in this lifetime? Any other aspects of that life? Whatever comes to mind.

R. I think . . . being influenced by others.

DR. F. All right, are there any other influences besides that—any physical characteristics or mental or emotional characteristics? What comes to mind? Your "yes" finger is moving.

R. Well, the only other things were that I was pulled backwards into the crevasse and . . . broke my back again . . . the back of my head was crushed in.

DR. F. Has that affected you up here in this lifetime?

R. Yes. Headaches starting in the back of my head . . . and back problems.

DR. F. Is there anything else that has affected you?

R. Ah . . . shudders run up and down my back. I often feel sensitive in my back when I'm in that situation.

DR. F. What situation?

R. A group decision.

DR. F. Any other ways?

R. [Deep sigh.] The love of outdoors . . . a fear of mountains maybe, or . . . rather the fury of a mountain . . . I'm somewhat fearful of a great challenge.

DR. F. Is there anything else that's important for you to know about that lifetime?

R. ["No" finger lifts.]

DR. F. Now I'm going to ask you to let go of those memories. Move to the next event that has to do with your problems with decisions. One . . . two . . . three . . . four . . . five. Where are you now?

R. I think in the West, maybe New Orleans . . . in fact, it is the West.

DR. F. What are you doing?

R. [Straightening up.] I'm driving a carriage . . . I'm dressed very elegantly . . . down a street.

DR. F. What is your name?

R. Edgar.

DR. F. Well, Edgar, what's your last name?

R. [Long pause.]

206

DR. F. At the count of three you will know. One . . . two . . . three. What came to mind?

R. Tyrone or something like that.

DR. F. What do you look like?

R. I think I'm tall and handsome and . . . I'm white.

DR. F. What color hair do you have?

R. Black hair.

DR. F. Do you have a moustache or beard?

R. No.

DR. F. How old are you, Edgar?

R. Twenty-seven.

DR. F. Are you married?

R. No.

DR. F. What are you wearing?

R. A brown hat . . . no, a black hat and a suit . . . an elegant kind of jacket with a pretty—pretty shirt with ruffles on it . . . very elegantly dressed . . . sort of flashy. [Looking very pleased with himself.]

DR. F. Where are you going?

R. I'm going to see someone.

DR. F. Tell me more.

R. First I thought I was going to a . . . like gambling—like to go gambling . . . and then I had an impression that ah . . . I was going to see a pretty girl.

DR. F. Now move ahead in time until you get there. One . . . two . . . three and what comes to mind?

R. Steamboat.

DR. F. And where are you now?

R. Well, there's a steamboat I've ridden, driven my carriage to this steamboat.

DR. F. Did you drive your carriage there alone?

R. No, I think someone's with me.

DR. F. Who's with you? Just take a look.

R. Pretty girl.

DR. F. What's her name?

R. Eileen.

DR. F. Do you know her well?

R. No . . . I think I'm just courting her . . . and we're walking to the steamboat.

DR. F. Now just move ahead in time to the next signifi-

cant event at the count of five. One . . . two . . .
three . . . four . . . five and what comes to mind?

R. They're gambling on the boat.

DR. F. And what are you doing?

R. I'm watching the game very intently. Everyone's
watching the game. [Deep sigh.] I'm being encouraged to gamble and I don't want to . . . encouraged by her.

DR. F. Listen to what she's saying. At the count
of three. One . . . two . . . three . . . what does
she say?

R. "All the men gamble and you can stand to make *so*
much money."

DR. F. How do you feel when she says that?

R. I feel I don't want to. But I want to be like all the
other men. I think I want to impress her . . . but I
don't want to gamble. [Sounding disgruntled.]

DR. F. Why is that?

R. I don't like gambling.

DR. F. Have you ever done it before?

R. No . . . now, I'm taking the dice—rolling the dice.
So I'm gambling!

DR. F. All right now, at the count of five go to the next
significant event. One . . . two . . . three . . .
four . . . five and what comes to mind?

R. There's an argument over the . . . game . . . I'm
arguing . . . I've lost and I'm arguing that they've
cheated me.

DR. F. That who's cheated you?

R. The gamblers.

DR. F. What's happening? Just tell me about it, step by
step.

R. [Long pause.] I was arguing and . . . and . . .
[His body flinches.] . . . I was stabbed in the back!
Another man came up behind me and grabbed me
and . . . and stabbed me in the back. [Breathing
very fast now.]

DR. F. Where in the back?

R. In the lower back. [His voice sounds weak—tired.]

DR. F. And what happened as he stabbed you?

R. [Puzzled.] I think I . . . I died.

DR. F. Let's ask your inner mind if you died. If you did, your "yes" finger will lift. If not, your "no" finger will.

R. ["Yes" finger trembles as it lifts.]

Still in a trance, Roger said that the poor decision he made in that lifetime was to gamble. As he put it, ". . . my inability to—not do what I wanted to do. It cost me my life!" He was "compelled" to comply because of his need to please others, to maintain his image. His inner mind indicated he had carried over that problem, too. I asked him if there was anything else from that life that was still affecting him in his current life. He paused and then blurted out, "My . . . not trusting women!" I asked him to concentrate on his breathing in order to calm him, as well as to give him a transition since he was beginning to show signs of fatigue. After a few minutes, I suggested that his subconscious mind take him to another of the six events that were responsible for his indecisiveness. I counted to five and asked him what he was aware of:

R. [Looking worried.] There's fog.

DR. F. Where are you?

R. In a boat.

DR. F. What kind of boat is it?

R. A fishing boat.

DR. F. Tell me about yourself.

R. I think I'm Greek.

DR. F. What do you look like?

R. Long hair . . . no moustache . . . very good physical shape . . . strong.

DR. F. How old are you?

R. Seventeen.

DR. F. Is the boat moving?

R. The boat's moving into the fog. [He begins to squirm.]

DR. F. Tell me what you're doing right now.

R. I don't think I want to go into the fog.

DR. F. Why is that?

R. [Deep sigh.] Because it's too dangerous.

DR. F. Why is it—

R. [Interrupting.] Stay out in—in the light.

DR. F. Well then, why are you going in?

R. Someone is urging me to go into the fog.

DR. F. Who is that?

R. I don't know.

DR. F. I'm going to count from one to three and on the count of three, you will know. One . . . two . . . three and who comes to mind?

R. My captain.

DR. F. Is this a large boat that you're on?

R. I think there's three of us on it.

DR. F. What is your name? What comes to mind?

R. I have no . . . kind of . . . something with a M . . .

DR. F. I'm going to count from one to three and on the count of three you will know what your name is. One . . . two . . . three and what comes to mind?

R. Moustache. [I thought to myself Greeks loved nicknames, even in those days!]

DR. F. So you don't want to go into the fog. But your captain says that you should go, is that it?

R. [Nods his head yes.]

DR. F. Do you say anything to the captain about the fog, Moustache?

R. I don't think so.

DR. F. Do you have a strong feeling about going into the fog?

R. I think it's wrong and dangerous. [The pulse in his neck quickens.]

DR. F. Why don't you say anything?

R. I think it's better to be brave . . . better to follow orders.

DR. F. All right, just move ahead in time to the next significant event at the count of five. One . . . two . . . three . . . four . . . five. What happens?

R. We hit some rocks and . . . and I was pitched out on my head . . . on the reef of rocks. [Grimacing as though in pain.]

DR. F. Tell me more about that.

R. I was pitched out on my head and my back . . .
   on some rocks . . . and they *grind* against me.
DR. F. What grinds against you?
R. The rocks . . . and the boat.
DR. F. The boat, too? What happens?
R. . . . and I died. [His voice fading.]

He explained under hypnosis that again his need to
please had superseded his own judgment. Again, he
found himself powerless to assert his needs and wishes.
He realized his life-long dread of fog originated in that
life, adding that he always checked weather conditions
before driving through areas where fog can be a hazard.
Nothing else from that life seemed to be affecting him
in his current one.

Checking with his finger signals, I found that Roger
had made another wrong (perhaps fatal, again?) decision. I asked his inner mind to go to that event. He grimaced and grabbed at his neck. He was experiencing so
much anxiety I had to give him calming suggestions and
moved him back to an earlier, neutral event. After a
few moments, I asked him where he was.

R. [Long pause.] I'm in a court . . . in France.
DR. F. Tell me what's happening.
R. There's a lot of jeering . . . people . . . arguing
   people.
DR. F. What are they arguing and jeering about?
R. They want to do away with the king.
DR. F. Why are you in court? What's going on?
R. Well, I mean in a court that's like a . . . I think I
   was . . . [Big sigh.] . . . maybe I—I'm wearing
   robes and have some kind of elevated position in the
   court . . . in France.
DR. F. What is your name?
R. Pierre.
DR. F. What's your last name, Pierre?
R. Rudin.
DR. F. Your inner mind is taking you to an event that is
   responsible for your problem up here in this lifetime.

211

To that event at the count of three. One . . . two
. . . three and what comes to mind?

R. I think I tried to please the people.

DR. F. Tell me what you mean by that.

R. There's a part of me that wanted to please . . .
other people . . . but my basic nature said to . . .
not to do that.

DR. F. Tell me more about the circumstances.

R. I think that I was feeling sorry for the people.

DR. F. What people?

R. The lesser and unprivileged . . . people.

DR. F. What happened?

R. Everybody was talking about doing away with the
king . . . doing away with the court. Ummm . . .
just a tremendous idealism about a better system.

DR. F. And how did you feel?

R. I felt in conflict.

DR. F. Why is that?

R. I felt loyal to my king and yet loyalty toward the
people.

DR. F. What did you say?

R. [Hesitantly.] I don't think I said anything.

DR. F. Go to the next significant event at the count of
five. One . . . two . . . three . . . four . . . five
and what comes to mind?

R. He gave ah . . . secrets to the Ragoons . . . ah
. . . somebody . . . that name came to mind.

DR. F. Somebody gave secrets to the Ragoons?

R. I think so.

DR. F. What does that mean? Can you explain that to
me?

R. Well, I'm not sure. I think they're opposing the king.

DR. F. Tell me more.

R. It was my judgment not to ah . . . to support
him . . .

DR. F. Who is he?

R. Philippe. He works for me.

DR. F. You decide not to support him. What is he
doing?

R. No . . . ah . . . I don't want to support him . . .
but I don't want to ah . . . to ah . . . expose him.

DR. F. So what do you do?

R. [Lowering his voice] Nothing.

DR. F. What is your decision at this point?

R. To do nothing.

DR. F. What is he doing?

R. I think he's giving information about the court.

DR. F. To whom?

R. A group of assassins.

DR. F. Tell me more.

R. His politics were not mine . . . and I didn't assert myself. I wasn't courageous. I should have stood up to him.

DR. F. What happened?

R. I got blackmailed into giving information. [Mumbling.]

DR. F. You, yourself, had to give information?

R. . . . or I'd be exposed.

DR. F. And then what happens? Move ahead in time and see what happens as a result of . . .

R. He talks . . . and exposed me . . . said *I* did it!

DR. F. What happened next?

R. Then I . . . [Wincing.] . . . was decapitated.

DR. F. Calm and relaxed . . . By whom?

R. By the king's men and . . . Philippe. He just stood there.

As Roger came out of hypnosis, he stretched his arms above his head. Then he collapsed back into the chair. He looked drained. His voice was drained. "I didn't realize what I was ready for!" We had run over thirty minutes. We only had time briefly to review how his decision had proved fatal—in each instance. I asked him to do some "homework" in the interval between sessions; to think back over each lifetime and see what role it played in his current life—and to write down these thoughts. We would examine them next time.

Two weeks later, Roger sprang up from his chair in the waiting room and strode quickly and confidently into my consultation room. Smiling broadly, he waved his two-page list. He had done his homework! With a great deal of energy in his voice, he said, "The list will have to wait—I want to tell you about all the *monumental* decisions I have made in these past two weeks." He crisply clipped them off. They ranged from his resigning from his teaching position at the college to buying a Dodge custom van and an exotic speedboat—for his brand new project—a movie on water skiing. I smiled and quoted, "If I get this problem solved, there'll be no stopping me!" He went on to tell me how "clear-headed" and relaxed he had been for the first time he could remember. How good it felt to look at a situation and know what he should do—and do it.

The energy in the room was almost crackling! His excitement and vitality had lit up his face—and was spilling over into his gestures, the force in his voice.

He picked up his list from the small teak table next to his chair and began reading. He examined the effects of his six lifetimes. He started with the last, the SS officer. He commented that he had died the same year he was born as Roger. "Not much time for recuperating!" Now he knew why he had always been intrigued with the Third Reich. He rubbed his chin, musing, "I had a weird experience near Munich. When I was there for the first time in 1968, I had an odd feeling—*déjà vu*—I felt as though I had been there before." He also was overwhelmed by anxiety—and couldn't understand why.

Since we had already looked at many of the aspects of his life as Tanakee, he quickly glossed over them. He sounded nostalgic as he spoke of his love of nature and mountains. He told me he loves skiing. His total distaste for gambling—even reluctance to play blackjack for a dime a chip with close friends—he traced to his existence as Edgar. He grinned. Looking guilty, he confessed, "I love to dress up and I have spent a great deal of money on an *outstanding* wardrobe." His fascination with politics and the clandestine maneuvering of rival power structures had been almost a hobby. This he attributed to his life in the court in France, and also to the German life. His voice became heavy as he talked about his recurrent back problems and headaches. No wonder!

214

"The common thread was my inability to assert myself and my need to please others at my own expense—often overriding my better judgment," he said.

Finally, he looked up from the last item on his list. He laughed and said, "Well, it will be interesting to see whether I change these things—I'll be so normal, I won't be able to stand myself!"

CHAPTER ELEVEN

❧

"I'm . . . Floating"

I have helped more than a thousand people die. All these deaths took place in my office. Sometimes during a fifty-minute session a patient dies three or even four times—all as different individuals. The individuals were the patient as he or she existed in previous lifetimes.

In most cases, the death experience is *the* event that is responsible for the person's symptoms and problems. Previous deaths have affected us in many ways—some obvious, some subtle. A fall from a cliff results in a phobia of heights. A drowning, fear of water. Crashing in a plane during a war engenders a fear of flying. Death from "consumption" results in chronic lung problems. Being bayoneted during sleep, insomnia.

I have observed many similarities and, occasionally, unique differences in these deaths. In preceding chapters, you have already seen how people describe their dying experience. In this chapter I share with you my observations of this event. A description of the interim between lifetimes, taken from my patients' fascinating accounts, will have to wait for a future publication. It is a book in itself!

The topic of death and dying is very emotion-laden for a great many people. Thanks to the work of researchers, the most prominent being Elisabeth Kübler-Ross, who has written *On Death and Dying* (New York: Macmillan Publishing Company, Inc., 1969), people are learning how to accept this aspect of living and are beginning to view death in a more positive way.

A few of my patients have shown great fright at the

prospect of going through their deaths under hypnosis. As one person asked, with genuine concern, "Do you think I might really die again?" We have to deal with the person's fears about death—as with fears about any traumatic event—before we can proceed. The trust and confidence my patients and subjects feel in me are the most essential and valuable aspect of our work together. It's an article of faith with me *never* to push them into something they cannot handle emotionally. I use various techniques to minimize the discomfort of relived physical or emotional pain. Besides these techniques, I must sometimes introduce people to their first death little by little. It has never been necessary to do this more than once. At times I have them watch their death on the movie screen of their mind, as though watching someone else experience it. Then, gradually, they allow themselves more participation as we go through it again. Finally, they experience it fully and completely.

All that I shall show you corroborates the findings of Raymond A. Moody, Jr., M.D. His book *Life After Life* (Covington, Georgia: Mockingbird Books, 1975) is based on interviews with over a hundred people who "died" during operations, illnesses or accidents. Their descriptions of their experiences before resuscitation are virtually identical to those of my patients under hypnosis—except that many of my patients recall events in the interim between lifetimes whereas Moody's do not. And for obvious reasons. His patients never made the transition complete. His patients chose not to die or were forced to return. Interestingly, the ancient *Tibetan Book of the Dead* also portrays many of the same events my patients and subjects have described.

One of the outstanding features in accounts of the death experience is that consciousness continues without a break. Also *every* patient or subject has described a release from physical and/or emotional pain at the moment of death—sometimes just before. If a person is dying of starvation, for example, there is no hunger. If the problem is lung congestion, often the first utterance is "I can breathe!"

217

A man in his thirties regressed to a life in which he murdered his adulterous wife. He was killed in the gas chamber for his crime.

L. [His face breaks out in beads of sweat.] I can't let them see that I care.

DR. F. Tell me how you feel. I won't tell them.

L. They're strappin' me in. [His body and voice trembling.]

DR. F. Go to the moment of your death at the count of three. One . . . Two . . . three.

L. It's all over with . . . peaceful.

The same patient in another life found himself in a foxhole during World War II.

L. [His body literally jerks. He grabs his neck.] . . . I died again . . . shot in the neck.

DR. F. How did it feel to die?

L. I just jerked.

DR. F. Do you feel anything?

L. No pain.

DR. F. Are you in the spirit body?

L. Um-hmm.

DR. F. How does that feel?

L. Oh, better.

In a past life, a young woman found her wagon train attacked by Indians who eventually scalped and raped her, leaving her to die. After a long silence she said:

C. I can see myself lying there.

DR. F. How do you feel?

C. It's over. (Her voice and face expressing relief.)

DR. F. Do you still feel the pain?

C. No.

DR. F. How do you feel?

C. (Smiling.) Fine . . . and that's it.

A woman describes the moment of her death. She has just been run over by a team of horses and a carriage.

DR. F. Now I'm going to ask you to go right to the moment of your death at the count of three. One . . .

two . . . three. Tell me what you're experiencing.

B. Just letting go.

DR. F. Tell me how that feels.

B. Ahh . . . it feels good.

DR. F. Tell me more.

B. I feel lighter . . . I don't feel heavy anymore.

DR. F. What else are you aware of?

B. I feel free.

DR. F. Where is your body?

B. On the ground.

DR. F. Where are you?

B. Just looking at it.

DR. F. From what viewpoint?

B. Just above it.

DR. F. How does your body look to you?

B. Looks rumpled.

DR. F. What emotions are you aware of?

B. Feel relief.

A woman in her twenties, with a weight problem, died of starvation in a previous life at the age of fifty-seven after being sick and very poor.

DR. F. How long have you had this problem of not eating because of money?

S. Oh, . . . a few years. I don't know how long . . . (Tears flowing down her face.) I don't feel well.

DR. F. Now I'd like you to move ahead a day. I'm going to count to five. One . . . two . . . three . . . four . . . five. Tell me what you are experiencing.

S. (Whispering.) I'm dying.

DR. F. Go to the moment of your death. One . . . two . . . three . . . four . . . five.

S. (Silence.)

DR. F. Margaret, what's happening to you now?

S. (Her voice stronger.) I'm dead . . . and I'm not hungry anymore.

DR. F. How do you feel now that you're dead?

S. I feel good.

One of the most moving death experiences I have witnessed evolved from a distressing series of events. A woman in her early thirties was exploring under hypnosis the origin of her panic on numerous occasions when she smelled a certain odor, especially if she was in a small room or enclosure at the time. She began our session by describing such an intense degree of panic that she was nearly fainting, very nauseous and was sick for several days afterward. She had innocently stepped into an elevator that had just been cleaned. The smell of disinfectant was still heavy in the air.

Her search for the cause of her reaction led us to Nazi Germany in the early nineteen forties. After describing a life filled with terrifying events, she found herself herded into a cattle car where she was almost crushed in the darkness by many other terrified Jews. The odor of excrement was stifling. There were no windows for air or light. After what seemed an eternity, but actually was three days, the train stopped. She stepped out into the blinding daylight and was led by guards to a place where she and the others were told to strip in preparation for bathing. There were rumors! There was fear! She was extremely frightened as she undressed, putting her shoes in one big pile of shoes of all kinds, her wedding ring in another pile, her dress in still another. Trembling, she followed the others into a large room.

DR. F. What is happening now?
A. They close the door.
DR. F. You're all in one room?
A. [Whispering.] Yes.
DR. F. Who closed the door?
A. The guards, I think.
DR. F. You say you're too tight to take baths. What do you mean?
A. Close together.
DR. F. Are you touching anyone? Are you that close, or could you spread your arms out?
A. I can move about. But it's crowded!
DR. F. Tell me what you see in this room.
A. No windows . . . the floor is cement. I feel it on my feet . . . it's cold . . .
DR. F. Is there any light?

220

A. No, it's very dark. There was a light, but it's not on.

DR. F. So you're in total darkness?

A. Yes.

DR. F. And now what are you thinking and feeling? Remaining really relaxed, deeper and deeper with each breath . . .

A. [Breathing hard. The pulse in her neck racing.]

DR. F. What are people doing?

A. I don't know. It doesn't seem very clear anymore.

DR. F. Now I'm going to ask you to just relax, breathe in golden light for the next minute or so, concentrate on breathing in golden light. I'm going to count again to ten. As I do, your inner mind will double the relaxation. Just concentrate on breathing in golden light, beautiful, relaxing golden light and by the time we reach ten you will be profoundly relaxed. You will be able to remember, experiencing freely. Meanwhile just relaxing deeper and deeper . . . one . . . two . . . three . . . four . . . five . . . six . . . seven . . . just relaxing so deeply with each count . . . eight . . . nine . . . ten. And now, Leah, tell me more about this room that you're in. What are the people doing?

A. I smell something again.

DR. F. What is it like?

A. Disinfectant. There's vents and it's coming from that.

DR. F. What did you say?

A. Vents. [Her body trembles.] People are starting to move away from them . . . crowding and . . . and getting away.

DR. F. How far are you from the vents?

A. Quite a way, but they've shoving back against me.

DR. F. What are they doing besides moving? Are they saying anything?

A. People are yelling and shouting and screaming.

DR. F. What are they saying as they yell and shout and scream?

A. I don't know.

DR. F. Listen and hear. I'm going to count to three, and hear what they say. One . . . two . . . three.

A. [Silence.]

221

DR. F. What do they say?

A. [Silence.]

DR. F. What comes to mind?

A. "Oh, no!" people say. And . . . and "My God!" some people say.

DR. F. What do you do? What are you doing?

A. I don't—I don't know. I don't have any sense of it.

DR. F. Now what are you aware of? What's happening now with the people?

A. I slipped and fell.

DR. F. How did that happen?

A. I just feel strange.

DR. F. Tell me about that. Tell me how you feel just before you slip and fall. What are you feeling and what are you thinking?

A. I'm engulfed in terror.

DR. F. Now what's happening?

A. Tangled mass of bodies . . . and excrement.

DR. F. Where are you?

A. I don't know.

DR. F. Just become aware of what you feel, what you're experiencing. Where do you feel you are in this tangled mass of bodies.

A. I feel I'm looking down on it. Now I just feel confused.

DR. F. Can you see?

A. Yes.

Occasionally patients weep after their death as they look down and see relatives grieving. The sadness is always for others, not for the person they were—no matter how traumatic their deaths. Rarely, they may be momentarily upset when they look down and see their body; however, within seconds they express relief. It is as though the release from the agony, and the newly experienced joy and ecstasy overcome the past suffering. For many, death is a rather gentle slipping into a different—better—state.

Almost all people experiencing dying under hypnosis use the word "floating" to describe the immediate bodily sensations after death. They feel themselves rising into the air and viewing the scene below. They report hearing loud noises—ringing, buzzing, celestial music. A few have experienced going through a tunnel with a light at the other end.

Almost universally, patients report being alone in the spirit state immediately after death. After the sensation of floating, often within a few seconds, the presence of spiritual guides or a "guardian angel" is felt. Many experience them as a bright light—but a light with a benign, loving essence—there to help. Sometimes, the transition is aided by more definitive entities. The person is often greeted by deceased relatives or friends and, in one case, by a faithful dog the person had owned years before. Many times this evokes an emotional reaction of weeping with joy.

Roger, whom you met in Chapter Ten, died during the jousting match.

R. Well, it's like a . . . a warmth went throughout my circulatory system . . . through my whole body . . . and I saw a white light and floated away.

DR. F. Tell me more about that. Where are you?

R. I was lying face down and then I floated face down . . . floated up and . . . at first, for about three feet . . . and then I floated upright . . . just floated away.

DR. F. What does that mean to you?

R. [Short laugh.] Well, it means I died.

DR. F. What's happening now?

R. Just relief. A feeling of warmth through my whole body and release in my body.

DR. F. What do you see?

R. [Smiling.] Well, I see the whole area. I can see everything.

Roger described another death, this one from a stabbing during an argument at the gaming table.

223

R. I'm already dead. I just . . . focused into a beam of light . . . and immediately was far happier, strangely enough . . . expansion and release . . . flying upward . . . to the light.

DR. F. Tell me more about it. Were you aware of your body as you were doing that?

R. I floated out of my body almost instantly.

DR. F. Did you feel any pain as you were being stabbed?

R. I felt a sharp pain in the back . . . ripping.

DR. F. And what came next?

R. The light.

DR. F. Tell me about the light. What was it like?

R. It was a burst of light that—that just hits on my— like I couldn't—couldn't see anything anymore, just the light, and it was small and then it expanded very quickly. I just floated up and expanded into the light.

DR. F. Did you have any feeling about the light other than it being a light?

R. Warm.

DR. F. It's warm in what sense?

R. It's warm . . . it's just physically warm.

DR. F. Do you have any other feeling about it?

R. It is friendly . . . and good.

DR. F. Is there anyone or anything there with you?

R. Friends of the family . . . waiting for me.

A young woman was in treatment for severe headaches. During the course of a past-life regression she went through the major events in a life as an aristocrat during the French Revolution. At the age of sixteen, she was captured by soldiers as she was escaping with her nanny at night. Her parents had already been arrested the day before. She describes the scene at the guillotine:

C. I'm kneeling down.

DR. F. Is anyone there with you?

C. The soldiers.

DR. F. Tell me what's happening now.

C. [Sounds of labored breathing.]

DR. F. What are your last thoughts?

C. Thinking how happy I was . . . how I wish I could

live . . . marry and have children. [Suddenly she jerks her head violently.]

DR. F. Where is your head now? And your body now?

C. . . . They're separated. [Sounding surprised.]

DR. F. What did it feel like when the blade struck your neck?

C. It's horribly painful.

DR. F. And now what are you experiencing?

C. [Long silence.] I'm not . . . sad anymore . . . feel happy.

DR. F. Are you still in your body?

C. No.

DR. F. Are you there by yourself in spirit form?

C. No, my guides have come. [Her face softens.]

DR. F. What do they say to you? What do they communicate to you?

C. They've come to take me home.

DR. F. How many are there?

C. Five.

DR. F. Do they look familiar to you?

C. Yes, of course.

DR. F. Why is that?

C. Because they're my guides. They're always there when I come home.

DR. F. They are the same ones who are always there?

C. Yes.

DR. F. Is anybody else there? Are other spirits whom you recognize other than your guides?

C. Yes, my parents.

DR. F. Do they communicate with you?

C. Yes. They help me know that they don't have any more pain.

Margaret, a woman in her mid-fifties, had suffered for years from a phobia of heights. Even as a child she had recurrent nightmares of falling, always awakening before she reached the bottom. Her husband had recently suggested a trip to Europe. Her reaction was panic and despair. How she would love to go. But flying was out of the question! We were hoping to solve the problem in time for her husband's vacation, a few months in the future.

This was a particularly intriguing problem because we had quite inadvertently discovered while working on another symptom that in a former lifetime she also had a phobia of heights. (It is not uncommon to see a symptom carried through several prior existences.)

After quite a lot of resistance to regressing, she found herself in a dirigible in the early nineteen hundreds. She was a young Dutchman, Hans, who was the navigator of an experimental military airship. A great deal of turbulence forced the dirigible off its course and out over the ocean. Lightning struck it. It burst into flames and broke in two. Horrified, Hans watched the captain and the other crew member tumble out as the craft started to fall. Clinging to a metal rigging, he said:

M. I'm hanging on to the frame . . .

DR. F. How do you feel?

M. Terrified. [Her face is contorted.]

DR. F. Tell me what's happening now.

M. Losing my grip . . . and I let go.

DR. F. How do you feel as you let go?

M. Falling . . .

DR. F. How does that feel?

M. It seems as though I'm falling very, very rapidly . . . and the water is coming closer and closer and I'm screaming . . .

DR. F. Do you have any thoughts as you scream?

M. I know I'm going to die . . . and I'm frightened. I don't like . . . I don't like it and the water is coming up very, very fast . . . and when I hit it my neck breaks.

DR. F. You feel that happening? How are you falling? What is your position?

M. Just sort of tumbling.

DR. F. What hits first?

M. My head.

DR. F. What are you aware of?

M. I think I was . . . I think it's over very fast.

DR. F. And now what are you aware of?

M. [Deep sigh.]

DR. F. What are you aware of now, Hans?

M. Oh, my body is sinking down into the water . . .

DR. F. Where are you? What are you aware of and where are you?

M. I'm just watching.

DR. F. Where are you watching from?

M. From under the water, beneath the water.

DR. F. What are you watching?

M. I'm just watching it float down, down, down . . . like a—like a rag doll.

DR. F. And now what are you aware of?

M. That I don't want to be there anymore.

DR. F. And what do you do?

M. I just leave . . . I just shoot up to the surface.

DR. F. And then?

M. And then I keep right on going.

DR. F. And how does that feel?

M. Fine. I can see . . . [Clears throat.] . . . I can see pieces of the wreckage floating on the water.

DR. F. And how do you feel about that?

M. Well, I'm . . . annoyed. It's a waste.

DR. F. Tell me more.

M. Oh, I don't know . . .

DR. F. Are you alone?

M. Yes, I . . . I . . . there are others but . . . um . . . we're not talking.

DR. F. Who are the others?

M. They're the—they're the crew.

DR. F. Are they there where you are?

M. They're . . . not there physically, but they're there . . . I know they're there.

DR. F. Can you see them?

M. No, but we can communicate.

DR. F. Is there anyone, anything else there?

M. No, we just . . . we're going somewhere else now.

DR. F. Where is that?

M. I don't know . . . but we're . . . we're all going.

Another woman patient died as an abbot in a contemplative monastery in Italy in the fifteen hundreds. At the moment of his death he said:

H. It's . . . peace.

DR. F. And what are you aware of?

H. Floating.

DR. F. Do you see anything?

H. It's like I am in . . . the universe. [Her voice is full of awe.]

DR. F. Can you see your body?

H. It's just like it's floating . . . and there's no pain, just floating.

DR. F. Are you alone?

H. It's like I'm going to meet someone. I'm alone but I don't . . . feel alone.

A few minutes after being clubbed to death, Becky, the young woman whose account was described in Chapter Two, experienced:

B. It's my family.

DR. F. Tell me what you see.

B. [Crying.] They're waiting for me.

DR. F. Why are you crying?

B. I'm happy.

DR. F. Tell me what you see—whom you see.

B. My sisters and my parents. [Whispering.] They must have been killed.

DR. F. How do they look?

B. [No answer.]

DR. F. Do they look as they did when they were alive?

B. Yeah.

DR. F. Do they look exactly like that?

B. More vaporous.

DR. F. What is their expression?

B. [Smiling.] They're welcoming me.

DR. F. Now is there anything or anyone else there, too? Look around and see.

B. There's a very bright light.

228

DR. F. Where is it?

B. Off in the distance.

DR. F. Tell me about it. Do you have any feeling about it?

B. It's warm. It's welcoming. [With a blissful expression on her face.]

DR. F. All right. Let's see if you go to it.

B. I'm still with my family.

DR. F. What are they doing?

B. Hugging me.

DR. F. Is there anyone else there?

B. No.

DR. F. And now what? What are you experiencing now?

B. Happiness.

A woman suffering from depression died of starvation in her last incarnation.

DR. F. Are you alone?

S. [Whispering.] No, there seems to be some people coming.

DR. F. Who are they?

S. Friends . . . and my mom.

DR. F. How do you feel when you see them?

S. Happy.

DR. F. Tell me about them.

S. They're hugging me.

DR. F. How do they look?

S. Well, my mother looks very old. I haven't seen her in a long time. But she doesn't wear glasses.

DR. F. Did she used to wear glasses?

S. Yes, and she . . . she says that she doesn't look the way I'm seeing her, but I have to get used to her.

DR. F. Is there anybody there whom you don't know?

S. There are a few that are there that I don't really know. But everything's fine.

DR. F. How are they dressed?

S. They have robes on. My mother's the only one with a dress on and an apron.

DR. F. What about your body? What is your body like?

S. It's not shriveled up like it was.

229

DR. F. Is it like a solid human body?

S. No, it's like I can see lights on my body. I don't really see anything other than a form—but I feel good.

My patients and subjects have often elaborately described what is done to their body after their spirit has floated way above it. For some time there can be an awareness of physical sensations in the deceased body—alternating with the consciousness experienced well outside the body. Patients have traced claustrophobia to being "buried alive," when actually—from their descriptions—they probably were dead. But their awareness and consciousness reverted back into the body. This occurs even after they witness the removal and burial of the body. Patients have commented on their funeral, sometimes expressing displeasure because of one aspect or another, such as a relative being absent. One woman, under hypnosis, traced her repugnance—nausea, in fact—to the aroma of roses. The scene was Nazi Germany and her body was being dumped into a trench with others. She realized that roses reminded her of the smell of her own and others' decaying bodies. Another patient traced the sensation of heat she feels when nervous to being cremated.

The alternation of the consciousness that is often experienced is shown by this excerpt from a male patient's transcript. His story of a fall from a cathedral roof was related in Chapter Seven:

M. Well, it's like people are putting something into the . . . wagon . . .

DR. F. What was that something?

M. It seems like they were dressed like soldiers.

DR. F. What were they putting into the wagon?

M. I don't know, it was stiff, I don't know what—why they would do that.

DR. F. What kind of thing was it?

M. Couldn't make out because I was . . . on the ground, I thought, this is where I viewed this from.

DR. F. You see them putting something stiff in the wagon?

230

M. Yes.

DR. F. What shape is it?

M. It's long like a man, like a . . . I don't know why they would be doing that . . .

DR. F. You don't know why they'd be doing that?

M. No, but whatever it is . . . well, it's just a . . . shutting down on the top and hauling it off. It had wheels.

DR. F. What did you say?

M. Shutting the top—it had like a . . . cover and two of them hauling it off.

DR. F. What are they hauling off?

M. A cart.

DR. F. But what are they hauling in the cart? What is that thing that they put in there? What comes to mind?

M. [Deep, prolonged sigh.] Oh, I see the inside of the cart, that's all . . . it looks like a long tunnel with a little light at the end.

DR. F. Do you feel as if you're in there now?

M. Yeah, but I'm—I'm not concerned about it.

DR. F. You feel like you're in there but you're not concerned?

M. Um-hmm. It's . . . now I see a blue light . . . now I see something unloaded . . . and I see men . . . carrying a . . . something to . . . this is when I see the blue.

DR. F. Now what's happening?

M. I just saw a man, like I was below in this cart again . . . they were holding the body, towards—toward the hole, toward me.

DR. F. You're in this hole and you're watching them bring this body?

M. In the hole I'm in.

DR. F. You're in a hole?

M. Below the cart.

DR. F. Where's the hole? Is it in the ground?

M. Yes.

DR. F. And now what?

M. I see two stone . . . things on each side of me and dirt . . . just stones lying on the dirt.

231

DR. F. On top of the dirt?

M. Um-hmm.

DR. F. Like a headstone, you mean?

M. No, like a . . . like the . . . one on each side.

DR. F. Now what are you aware of? What colors are you aware of, if any?

M. Sort of blurred colors. I see deep blue. I see . . . that heavy blue sky above me . . . the men in the uniforms leaning over and throwing . . . dirt in . . . gray uniforms.

DR. F. Is it as though you're outside watching them fill in the grave?

M. No, I'm inside.

DR. F. But you can see them there in some kind of way.

M. It blurs.

A young teenage boy was affected by a former death in a Nazi concentration camp. After being gassed, his body was thrown into an open ditch. Yellow bulldozers pushed mounds of dirt onto all the bodies. He felt the dirt covering his face. Three years ago he had developed a severe facial tic, which was his reason for seeking help. Dirt caked on his face when he was helping friends put in a post-and-hole fence. He was unable to wash it off for several hours. Under hypnosis he went back to that event and then back further to the original event—at the concentration camp. His tic was caused by his smelling gas and contorting his face as he dropped to the floor of the showers. The caked dirt reminded him at a deep subconscious level of the time he was gassed to death.

Several patients have reported their spirits' mocking of the assailants or murderers. The following brief excerpt shows an instance of this kind of behavior. A woman patient traced her allergy that affected her lungs and sinuses back to a death in a jungle.

H. I'm in a jungle and it's very hot.

DR. F. What are you doing in the jungle?

H. I'm pursued by some cannibals . . . they want to eat me.

DR. F. Tell me about yourself.

H. I'm a tall, strong warrior, very black.

DR. F. Did you say you were a warrior?

H. A warrior.

DR. F. And you're very black.

H. Very black and I'm very strong. [With pride in her voice.]

DR. F. What is your name?

H. Wanna.

DR. F. Wanna, you said you were being pursued? Tell me about that.

H. There's other warriors chasing me through . . . through the jungle and it's very hot, humid . . . water's running down my body. [Breathing fast.]

DR. F. Do you know who the people are who are pursuing you? Have you seen them?

H. They're other black . . . warriors . . . from another tribe. I want to say Utse tribe.

DR. F. Utse?

H. I . . . [Gasping.] . . . I'm just running and I can't catch my breath.

DR. F. Why is that?

H. The air seems too oppressive like there's gas or . . . very dank . . . and I trip and fall into some quicksand and . . . and I'm being swallowed up. [Panicky.]

DR. F. Now where are the others who were pursuing you?

H. I can hear them yelling, shouting, and I'm struggling in this quicksand . . . and I can't get out and I keep struggling and struggling.

DR. F. What are you aware of now?

H. It's in my throat. [Voice straining.] It's just coming up to my nose, I just can't . . . I'm just going. [Sweat breaking out on her face.]

DR. F. What are your thoughts?

H. What a way—way to go. No . . . honor. [Gasping for breath.]

DR. F. And now where is the quicksand?

H. It's going into my nose. It's horrid . . . smell and putrid . . . I keep struggling and the weight is so heavy on me . . . [Struggling.] I can't move. [Grimacing.]

DR. F. Can you breathe at this point?

H. No, I'm . . . I finally give up . . . and just sink.

DR. F. What are you experiencing as you sink?

H. Peace. [Her whole body relaxes.] I can hear my heart pound in my ears and I just feel that my nostrils and mouth . . . and it's just got this gritty, gritty sand . . . it kind of burns and . . . it's fading away and I'm overcome with peace and I finally just give up. [Her face is peaceful.]

DR. F. And then what happens?

H. And then I die.

DR. F. And now what are you aware of?

H. Relaxation. It seems like I'm momentarily watching myself sink and then I see warriors come and I . . . it looks like my spirit is laughing, like I finally beat them out. [Smiling broadly.]

DR. F. Are you aware of your spirit?

H. No, and my spirit doesn't stay long. It just stays there for a moment and watches the warriors and feels amused that they didn't catch him, catch me . . . and then I float away.

I am including the next excerpt from a transcript because it is one of the most unusual experiences a patient has described (so far!). It gives us a view of the death event from the other side, from the viewpoint of a spirit describing another's death.

Margaret, whom you met earlier in this chapter, found that several lifetimes were contributing to her phobias of flying and of heights.

Under hypnosis, she regressed into a lifetime as a young male Oriental, Wong-Tu. She described an extremely primitive existence. Wong lived in a thatched hut with an aged, wizened and deeply beloved grandmother. One day there was simply nothing left to eat. Others in the village could not share their dwindling reserves. Wong crossed a footbridge strung between two mountains and crept down the mountainside into an-

other village. He quickly grabbed a prize—a chicken—
and dashed up the mountain again, with outraged vil-
lagers in hot pursuit. He began running across the swaying footbridge, a chicken in one hand, the other gliding
along the rope. The small pieces of bamboo that com-
prised the flooring were dangerously slippery because of
a heavy fog. Much to Wong's horror the men stopped
their pursuit and started shaking the bridge with all
their might. He looked down and saw a drop of thousands of feet. Formerly he had no fear when he crossed
the bridge on numerous occasions. I ask him how he
feels now.

M. I'm frightened . . . I . . . I let go of the chicken,
so that I can hold on with both hands . . . but I . . .
I'm . . . my foot slips from under me . . . and I'm
hanging there from the . . . from the rope on one
side, on the left side of the bridge and I . . .

DR. F. What are your feelings as this is happening,
Wong?

M. I'm beginning to scream for help and they just keep
shaking . . . the ropes on the bridge . . . and I can
see way, way down. It's all rocks, way down, so far
down rocks and water . . .

DR. F. What are you thinking now, Wong?

M. [Shaking violently.] I'm falling . . .

DR. F. How do you feel as you're falling?

M. I'm just falling . . . [Deep sigh.] . . . seems like
I'm falling forever.

DR. F. What thoughts go through your mind as you're
falling?

M. I'm . . . I don't know . . .

DR. F. Now what's happening, Wong?

M. I can see my body falling but I'm . . . I'm not
afraid anymore. It's as though I were floating.

DR. F. Just watch your body and tell me what you see
happening to it.

M. It falls onto the rocks . . .

DR. F. How do you feel as you see that happening?
What are you aware of?

M. I . . . my face is down on the rocks but I don't—I don't feel anything. I was very . . . I was very afraid, but not . . . I'm . . . I'm just surprised.

DR. F. Where do you feel like you are?

M. I don't know where I am. [Puzzled.] I'm just . . . I'm just floating around. The body was falling but I stopped falling. I feel like . . . [Long pause.]

DR. F. And now I'd like you to move forward in time to the next significant event. Staying in the spirit state . . . one . . . two . . . three . . . four . . . five. What are you aware of?

M. I'm looking at my grandmother and she's there, waiting for me to come . . . and there's no food . . . and . . . she sort of sits in a squatting position and puts her hands around her knees. She's very old and she's hungry and now she won't . . . won't live much longer because she doesn't have food. She doesn't have me to help her . . . and that makes me feel sad . . . but I don't think I'll . . . I don't think she really minds . . . because she'll be . . . [Deep sigh.] . . . she's ready to leave that world anyway.

DR. F. Are you with anyone in the spiritual state?

M. No.

DR. F. Any friends?

M. No.

DR. F. I'd like you to move forward to the next significant event, just staying in your spiritual state. One . . . two . . . three . . . four . . . five. Where are you now and what are you experiencing?

M. Nothing.

DR. F. Does anything come to mind?

M. No.

DR. F. Speak out your thoughts. What are you experiencing?

M. I don't know . . . regret.

DR. F. Tell me what you mean by that.

M. I don't know.

DR. F. I'd like you to move forward to the time when you are with your grandmother again. One . . . two . . . three . . . four . . . five. What are you experiencing?

M. Well, she's . . . I'm waiting for her and she's . . .
she is dying of starvation but she's . . . I can communicate with her.

DR. F. What have you communicated so far with her?

M. I tell her not to be afraid and not to worry and that
we'll be together soon, and she says that she will be
happy to be with me . . . that's all.

DR. F. Go to the moment of her death at the count of
five. One . . . two . . . three . . . four . . . five.
Tell me what you're seeing now.

M. She . . . I see her standing beside her own body
looking down at it . . . and I call to her and she turns
away from it and she moves in my direction very rapidly as though she were on a . . . oh . . . some
. . . just moves very rapidly right through, through
space.

DR. F. How does she look?

M. She looks much better than . . . she looks the same
as she did before . . . she looks the same as she did
. . . before I stole the chicken . . . before she died
of starvation. She's still old, but she . . . she looks
happy and she's smiling and she has her hands out to
me . . . and sort of . . . can't really touch her but
I can see her.

DR. F. Do you communicate with her?

M. Yes.

DR. F. Tell me about that. How do you communicate
and what do you communicate?

M. Oh, we communicate our thoughts.

DR. F. What are you saying or what are you communicating to her?

M. Just that I'm glad that she's with me. Then I told her
about the chicken because she never did know what
happened to me . . . why I didn't come back.

DR. F. What is she communicating to you?

M. She says that we'll be together now, always. She's
smiling.

DR. F. Are you alone, the two of you?

M. Yes.

DR. F. And now what's happening?

M. We're just sort of moving along together now.

DR. F. How are you moving?

M. Just moving.

DR. F. Slowly or rapidly?

M. Slowly now that she's here.

Many of my patients have told me that going through the death experience has a profound and awakening effect on them. It was a peak experience, a highlight in this life. For those who believe in life after death, it was reassuring, almost constituting proof. It was often awe-inspiring. For those who didn't believe, it often triggered a chain reaction, with a shaking of old convictions and ending with dramatic changes in basic philosophical beliefs. People were moved to read everything they could find to try to substantiate their own personal experience. For some it created conflicts with their religious convictions. These people resolved these conflicts by growing—thinking for themselves. They felt comfortable and relaxed, as they realized they wouldn't be damned as sinners if they began to question.

For most, it dispelled the fear of death, a fear that seems really to be the fear of the pain of dying, the fear of leaving loved ones behind and, ultimately, the fear of the unknown. After experiencing their own deaths, their fears dissipated. In fact, many reported preferring the afterlife to their present lives!

The feature that emerged most consistently was the inner, personal feeling of survival after death. As one patient put it, "It's wonderful to know that when we die, it's just another beginning."

✖

CHAPTER TWELVE

"We Live Many Lifetimes"

The work that has been presented in this book generates many questions. Hopefully it answers many.

The first question that we must consider is, are the patients and subjects deliberately lying? Are they putting on an act? If so, most should be nominated for Academy awards! I have listened to and watched people in past-life regressions under hypnosis for thousands of hours. I am convinced there is no deliberate, nor conscious attempt to deceive. The tears, shaking, flinching, smiling, gasping for breath, groaning, sweating and other physical manifestations are all too real.

The next question that comes to mind is, could the former lifetime that is experienced be an elaborate fantasy the patient believes is reality? It could be that the human mind, being the remarkable "computer" it is, is able to take symptoms from this life and come up with a very realistic "former lifetime" that accounts for the problem. So far that question has not been *definitively* answered in my own mind. I am doing research on lives in which there are birth dates or death dates and other concrete "evidence." This research will be reported in a future publication. Excellent research on this question has been done by Ian Stevenson (*Twenty Cases Suggestive of Reincarnation*, New York, American Society for Psychical Research, 1966). He presents twenty well-documented cases from various areas of the world.

At this point I feel that the end result, in terms of remission of symptoms, is almost conclusive proof. I view past-life therapy as virtually identical with hypnoanalysis that regresses the person back to significant events in the current life. Relatives, and the patient himself or herself, very often establish the validity of the relived events, once they are brought to light. Patients are often surprised—and delighted—when their birth experience, for example, is verified by their mothers' accounts. I see a previous life as essentially just another point on the continuum.

In thinking back over the regressions I have participated in, it is notable that the lives that are relived are usually unlikely candidates for fantasies. Patients and subjects most often experience very prosaic, humdrum, dreary past lives, totally lacking in glamour. Still, we cannot completely dismiss the possibility that these regressions are pure fantasy just because the lives do not fit a stereotype of what a fantasy *should* be like.

Another question that arises is if we do live again and again, what is the purpose of reincarnation? A woman who came for a past-life regression is the source for an answer. She recounted a peak experience she had:

At the moment of my son's birth, a natural childbirth, a voice spoke to me. It explained why we're here—the reason why we're here, what life is all about, the truth. And the truth is that we're all on a path back to God and we live many lifetimes. We live by the law of Karma which dictates, in effect, that we have to pay off the debts from our past lives. Once we die, we look back on how we lived that life. We decide whether or not . . . *we* are the judges of how we lived that life. We look to see where we failed. Maybe it's like a stylus constantly recording. Our soul is constantly having the stylus going, recording our deeds, our thoughts, our actions, whether or not we're hurting anybody—and that's what it's all about. Love is how we treat others, by word and by deed. After we cross over, we examine how we lived our last lives. We see where we failed and where we maybe made some gains. Then we choose our next life. *We* choose our next life, how we are going to be able to make up for where we didn't quite make it in our last lives. And this voice told me this in a split second!

This explanation is not original. In fact it is the usual view of reincarnation—the perfecting of one's soul. My patients' descriptions of the knowledge and training they experience during the interim between lifetimes confirm the explanation that was given to the woman above at her son's birth. Interestingly, she had not read or heard anything about Karma. It was totally new to her then. That experience profoundly affected her and she has studied in this area since then. The issue of Karma and the past-life origin of symptoms and problems has been dealt with at length in Gina Cerminara's books on the Edgar Cayce life readings (*The World Within*, New York, Wm. Morrow and Company, Inc., 1957; *Many Lives, Many Loves*, New York, Wm. Morrow and Company, Inc., 1963; *Many Mansions*, New York, Wm. Morrow and Company, Inc., 1950 New American Library). Her conclusions are very much in keeping with my findings.

The next question that might occur is, why do we keep coming back with the same people? Eastern philosophers and metaphysicians would suggest—and I, too, find it true in my work—that sometimes we have problems from past lifetimes to work out with those people. This is also the main theme of Dick Sutphen's exciting book, *You Were Born Again to Be Together* (New York: Pocket Books, 1976). In my work, one of my patients found that in his former life he murdered his wife after she flaunted extramarital affairs in his face. He stays with her now, despite tremendous marital difficulties. He owes her a debt. It seems that people who have worked out their problems often stay together because of a bond of love or friendship. One woman wanted to explore a previous lifetime with her daughter with whom she has had a fine, close relationship. In a recent past life they were loving sisters. Looking back over the regressions I have witnessed, the general rule seems to be when there is a good relationship now, there usually has been a positive relationship in previous lives. This is particularly true for fairly recent past lifetimes because problems from earlier lives together have been worked out. There is an obverse side to this coin. If there is disharmony now, a poor relationship is generally discovered in the past.

The ultimate question is, who are we? During the past years, as a result of working with past-life regressions, I have changed—and continue to change—my religious and philosophical beliefs. I no longer feel comfortable being an agnostic. I see things very differently and believe that this one life cannot be all there is or has been. I now feel very much in agreement with the tenet of many major religions of the world. We are the sum total of all that we have been before.